What people a ‖‖‖‖‖‖‖‖‖‖‖‖
M000204955

Tomorrow's Jobs Today

In today's data-driven, fast-changing world, *Tomorrow's Jobs Today* gives business leaders and job seekers alike a solid overview of many complex technology trends. This book helps surface the issues everyone needs to be aware of and provides food for thought on how they might be navigated as we head into a new decade.
Gregory L. Steinhauer, President, American Life Inc.

Information is the currency that fuels and funds the Digital Transformation journey. *Tomorrow's Jobs Today* manages to capture a set of leadership perspectives that, while diverse, share an essential characteristic for the future of transformative work: leveraging information as one's most valuable asset.
Peggy Winton, CEO, Association for Intelligent Information Management AIIM

If you want to stay successful, you have to embrace and adapt to changes. *Tomorrow's Jobs Today* shows you how those challenges can be both enlightening and empowering.
Jim Dodson, SVP, Iron Mountain

In a world often seized by ever-accelerating change, *Tomorrow's Jobs Today* has brilliantly identified, captured, and recounted liberating insights for success from a broad range of global information governance and technology professionals. There will always be challenges, but for those willing to look, the opportunity is abundant. The Information Age remains an ever-growing frontier awaiting each new wave of pioneers.
Seth Williams, President, MER Conference

This is an empowering and beautifully written book that will surely guide the reader to find a place in this quickly changing Information Age, where they can thrive and contribute to the greater good.

Dr. Angela Bair Schmider, M.S., Ph.D., Massachusetts General Hospital and Harvard Medical School

The authors bring together the voices of leading thinkers, exploring the critical themes that will dominate the years to come. Entertaining interviews reveal the best paths forward for professional development and the impending social, political, and ethical challenges of tomorrow. This is an important book.

Alex Panagides, CEO, mxHero

Tomorrow's Jobs Today brings together an impressive group of professionals sharing their wisdom and career advice from the cutting edge of technological advancement today. These insights will inevitably bolster your career path, and the combined knowledge of so many brilliant folks in one volume is staggering. I recommend this book for anyone who is pushing or looking to push their organizations into the future.

Nick Inglis, Executive Director of Content & Programming, ARMA International

This book is an excellent read for just about everyone trying to make sense of the ever-increasing pace of change going on around them. The interviews conducted in each chapter help ground and explain how others have harnessed these rapid changes for their personal fulfillment and most importantly for the greater good of humanity. For those feeling anxious over the stability of their roles, ponder this book and reap the wisdom presented.

John Isaza, Esq., FAI, Cofounder Information Governance Solutions

Stepping away from the mush of data that sometimes arrives through surveys, *Tomorrow's Jobs Today* goes straight to the people creating the future world of work. Read this book; go interview a few visionaries yourself; help shape the world to come.

Andy Watson, Head of School, Albuquerque Academy

Tomorrow's Jobs Today

Wisdom and Career Advice from
Thought Leaders in AI, Big Data,
Blockchain, the Internet of Things,
Privacy, and More

Tomorrow's Jobs Today

Wisdom and Career Advice from
Thought Leaders in AI, Big Data,
Blockchain, the Internet of Things,
Privacy, and More

Rafael Moscatel
with Abby Moscatel

BUSINESS
BOOKS

Winchester, UK
Washington, USA

JOHN HUNT PUBLISHING

First published by Business Books, 2021
Business Books is an imprint of John Hunt Publishing Ltd., No. 3 East St., Alresford,
Hampshire SO24 9EE, UK
office@jhpbooks.com
www.johnhuntpublishing.com
www.johnhuntpublishing.com/business-books

For distributor details and how to order please visit the 'Ordering' section on our website.

The opinions expressed by the interviewees in this book are their own and do not necessarily
reflect those of their employer.

Design: Stuart Davies

UK: Printed and bound by CPI Group (UK) Ltd, Croydon, CR0 4YY
Printed in North America by CPI GPS partners

We operate a distinctive and ethical publishing philosophy in
all areas of our business, from our global network of authors to
production and worldwide distribution.

Contents

Part III Relationships Matter   115

For our children,
from their employees.

Forward

Our brain is wired to make sense of the world.

It scans the environment for any and all things novel, matching what it finds to an internal threat matrix.

It kicks the job of making sense of it upstairs, where a middle manager fits the impression to the best fitting narrative about who, what, where, when, and how.

If the impression fits a survival narrative, the middle manager hits the panic button, initiating a fight, flight, freeze, or feign/appease response. In rapid succession, our brain floods our entire body with adrenaline and other stress hormones, our heartbeat quickens, vascular system contracts, field of vision narrows, and so on.

However, if the impression fits an opportunity narrative, the middle manager hits the desire button, initiating a consideration or pursuit response.

Sensing no immediate threat and plausible upsides, the middle manager kicks it up to the chief executive officer to decide what will likely happen next and what to do about the commotion.

For the most part, this has worked pretty well for human beings. However, the process comes with a few exceptions and variables.

Delphic Curse - Most predictions are simply wrong. Digging deeper, those predictions that most people consider plausible are often the most errant. And the most implausible or far-fetched predictions often turn out to be most accurate. But, so what? Nobody believes them!

The More Things Change - To update the old and somewhat cynical French proverb, amidst our times of great change, a surprising number of things stand unchanged, immutable. Of course, most of these things hide in plain sight and require

1

"piercing the veil of tranquilized obviousness."

Shut-down Syndrome - Rapid change of environments overwhelm our brains' ability to make sense. Unless we take measures to counteract this response, our brains will compel us to choose the familiar or mediocre option or to avoid criticism. In part, we can avoid this by learning from others about how they navigated the vagaries and vicissitudes of their lives.

Uneven distribution - The future arrives unevenly distributed. Some of us have already immigrated to the world of hyper-connectivity and intelligent assistance, putting surfboards into water with the aim of surfing the next trillion-dollar wave of innovation, wealth creation, and disruption. Some of us see the winds of change on the distant horizon, believing that we have the luxury of two to three years to make a change. Many believe their window has already opened and closed. Just like jumping from a skyscraper, they feel there's zero doubt they'll hit the ground. Still, others of us don't see anything in our way, nor do we believe that anything bad will happen. We'll continue to just keep on, keeping on. Who's right? "Well, even if I knew, no one would believe me!"

Opportunity and Innovation Diffusion Curves - We can count on the fact that entrepreneurs and technology enterprises will continue to invent, innovate, and disrupt the status quo. For the foreseeable future, there will be jobs and careers for speeding the introduction and adoption of new technologies and building operationalization capabilities (accountabilities, workflows, and systems). Experimenters, early adopters, early majority, late majority, and laggards will all have jobs to do. However, we will discover that we must now cycle quickly through all those jobs.

And that's where this book can aid both the young professional and the seasoned executive.

Rafael and Abby have interviewed dozens of accomplished and forward-thinking industry leaders and innovators to present their observations about several technologies and trends.

This alone will give you tons of insight and background on a burgeoning array of developments.

However, most of what they will say about YOUR future might miss the mark by miles. That's a good thing: it will be only through your unique perspective that you will see opportunities that hide in plain sight of YOUR world.

What remains the same amidst all this change? Decency, dignity, fairness, discernment, and flexibility.

Now more than ever, the world rewards those who parlay small wins into stupendous gains, who play to their individual strengths, who learn how they learn, and who know that most of what's good in the world resulted from high performing teams and their leaders.

So be that guy or gal.

As you read these interviews, pay attention to more than just the particular concepts and technologies.

Pay attention to the narratives, the story logic, and themes that each interviewee brought to their situations and opportunities.

Pay attention to how they made sense of THEIR world, considering their social and cultural norms as well as their particular beliefs, talents, and lucky breaks.

Dive head-first into their narratives, immersing yourself in their world, paying rapt attention to the whispers and nudges of YOUR intuition and Greater Imagination.

If you so choose, read between the lines, discerning their Beliefs (cause effects) and Context of Being (who must one be, then and there, to have had those experiences and recollected or abstracted those experiences *in these words that I now read?*).

As you get a sense of their worldview, have them coach or mentor you about your current situation, goals, and challenges.

As you read these interviews, also have them read you: Use them as prompts or cues of your Greater Imagination or self.

As you read about their particular job, know that it's possible it may soon no longer exist as an economically sustainable engagement.

But do know that the ultimate meta job is about how to design the ideal job, the job that fits you, hand and glove. The job that plays to your strengths, the one that demands your personal excellence and that you will find worth doing even if it does not pay top bracket salary!

So, your shot on goal here is simple: learn how to design your ideal job for *tomorrow*, using the sense-making criteria and narratives of those whose shoulders you stand on *today*.

Michael Jay Moon
CEO, GISTICS and Gratitude Games
Author, *Firebrands: Building Brand Loyalty in the Internet Age*

Acknowledgments

We tend to credit the knowledge we've acquired throughout the years as either a direct benefit of our education or an indirect blessing of life's humbling experiences. Yet, whether we studied at Oxford or the School of Hard Knocks, we recognize that gaining wisdom is worthier than any mastery of facts, figures, and skillsets.

Wisdom is the reasoned synthesis and acute application of knowledge to life's greater goals and meaning. It's a gift and collective treasure that requires years if not generations of blood, sweat, and tears, trial and error, heroism and tragedy to be honed, survive judgment, and be passed along to new stewards. Wisdom travels from mother to son, father to daughter, teacher to pupil, from master to fellow to apprentice. It is sweetest when given freely and most bitter when taken for granted. We can't put a price on this invisible commodity. We can only hope to repay those charitable enough to have shared it with us.

It was in this spirit of seeking wisdom that we sought out some of our brightest colleagues in emerging fields like blockchain, artificial intelligence, and privacy for the lessons outlined in this book of in-depth interviews. The goal was to enrich our own perspectives and those of you, the reader, with the intimate reflections of successful thought leaders helping to shape *Tomorrow's Jobs Today*. These trailblazers and their exceptional careers represent some of the finest pedagogical examples of the marriage of education and experience found across the globe. Their altruistic motives for freely sharing these insights with us underscore their professionalism and serve as documented proof that the best minds always lead by example.

We want to extend our sincere gratitude to each of the visionary business and civic leaders around the world who shared their time, guidance, and career insights to make this book possible.

5

Thank you to our colleagues and friends, including Michael Jay Moon, Dr. Jones Lukose Ongalo, Andrea Kalas, Miguel Mairlot, Ashish Gadnis, Priya Keshav, Amb-Dr. Oyedokun Ayodeji Oyewole, Markus Lindelow, Dr. Ulrich Kampffmeyer, Dr. Anita Allen, Douglas C. Williams, Kevin Gray, George Socha, Esq., Dr. Katrina Miller Parrish, Mark Patrick, John Danenberger, Esq., Dr. Anand Rao, April Dmytrenko, Patrick Sweeney and Erick Swain.

Thank you to the Schmider family, Allison Lloyd, Kathryn Keene, Sean Conley, Sharon Ware, and Nick Paonessa.

To the stellar team at John Hunt publishing, we thank you for believing in our book.

Most importantly, we thank our own beacons of wisdom, our loving parents, Dr. Raymond and Eleanor Moscatel, the late Lisa Bair, and Charles and Heide Bair.

Introduction

"As technological breakthroughs rapidly shift the frontier between the work tasks performed by humans and those performed by machines and algorithms, global labour markets are undergoing major transformations. These transformations, if managed wisely, could lead to a new age of good work, good jobs and improved quality of life for all, but if managed poorly, pose the risk of widening skills gaps, greater inequality and broader polarization."

Klaus Schwab, The Future of Jobs Report

It's every job seeker's dream to land both a financially and intellectually rewarding position doing something that they love. Or at least like! Yet these days, even amidst the abundant opportunities of the Information Age, folks of all skill levels continue to struggle with the best approach to a happy and successful vocation. Business models are transforming the job market so rapidly that even the most accomplished executives and educated employees suffer from anxiety over the stability of their roles. They must routinely prove their intrinsic value to their superiors and define their personal brand within their organization. For new graduates and those looking to make a big career transition, the reality of a continually shifting corporate landscape can feel almost paralyzing. The emergence of impersonal human resource tools like artificial intelligence in hiring practices has compounded traditional fears underlying the search for our rightful place in the new digital workplace.

There are plenty of recruiters, human resource professionals, and resources like *The Future of Jobs Report* quoted in the epigraph above that employ statistics and academic research to explain the modern workforce. These factoids are interesting, but only those with practical, first-hand experience can adequately convey the nuances of *what it means* to be and fulfill the responsibilities of a CIO, Blockchain Banker, Archivist, or Data Scientist. Profiles of today's business leaders regularly serve up softball interview questions that don't help us fully understand the big why behind the *how I got here* question. They rarely investigate how their subjects think about specific issues impacting their chosen fields. This book reflects the sobering perspectives of executives who sit on the firing line of board rooms and who also know their way around a server room. These interviews enable us to walk a mile in their shoes while exposing us to the exciting technology trends responsible for creating the workforce demands we see emerging today.

How do we discover where *our* contributions belong in this brave new world? How do we discern what work *we* should train for and exactly where *we* should perform it? What kinds of jobs are out there today, and what will they look like in the near distant future for us? Will they be there tomorrow, or even by the time you finish this book? Perhaps envisaging answers to these questions aren't so complicated at all. Maybe they're right under our noses and spelled out on the next few pages.

Indeed, the reasons for today's job anxiety and uncertainty aren't driven entirely by science fiction inspired fear of robots and automation. Those may be fun hypotheticals with a certain truth to them. Our visceral worries about our future job prospects are more aptly rooted in the reality that we don't do a very good job explaining what we do to each other. That's partly because, as a result of the pace of technology, tomorrow's work doesn't look much like yesterday's stack and probably never will. The bigger reality is that we're all so preoccupied with our professional goals (and devices) that we rarely sit down to thoughtfully communicate our priceless wisdom about our work outside of occasional mentoring programs or when writing a new job description.

Like most of us who grew up in or who were born in this Information Age, we've learned early on in our careers that we can't expect to develop and survive professionally, let alone thrive if we get too comfortable in our own silos. Our ideas will get stale, our skillsets will grow old, and our energy to adapt will precipitously decline. That familiar yet often overused maxim, "do what you love," while a historically useful antidote, isn't nearly enough to carry us over the finish line in today's corporate rat race. While we don't need to finish first technically, we should want to be in the right lane for as much of the journey as possible. That journey is most rewarding when it is equipped not merely with knowledge and experience but with the shared wisdom of proven leaders.

In these chapters and industry stories, we reveal the origins of those crafted insights and three strategic themes common to each of these visionary leaders: One - *How gaps (weaknesses) can become opportunities;* Two - *How less is often more*; and Three - Why, above all else, our *Relationships Matter* now as much as our credentials.

This book is for the new graduate, the professional between jobs and the doting parents desperate to get their "brilliant" but lazy kid out of the basement. It's also for senior corporate leaders seeking an intimate understanding of the changes abounding in their organizations. It's for the manager who wants to inspire and encourage professional development. And it's for every knowledge worker out there who wants to leverage technology and information governance to reduce risk, generate revenue, and improve customer experiences.

Tomorrow's Jobs Today is not for those who cower in the face of disruption. It's a resource for smart people like you who recognize the jobs of the future are very much here today and ours to adapt to. By absorbing the perspectives, challenges, and solutions of those deeply in love with and accomplished in these new careers, we can help ourselves, our friends, and our employees transform anxiety over a job search, job loss, or just the winds of change into hope, understanding, and opportunity.

Part I Gaps are Opportunities

"The Chinese use two brush strokes to write the word 'crisis.' One brush stroke stands for danger; the other for opportunity. In a crisis, be aware of the danger—but recognize the opportunity."
John F. Kennedy

The convergence of technology and the rule of law is expected to intensify over the coming years. It's a paradigm shift that will force organizations of all sizes, private and public, across all verticals, to balance a world ripe with innovation with an evolving universe of risk and regulatory pressure. Employers and their workforces will be inclined to adapt to this dynamic new digital landscape in their personal and professional lives. Like every era before it, the individuals who lead the way will separate themselves from the pack by identifying, engaging in, and fostering the right opportunities wherever they reveal themselves.

However, edging out rivals and birthing the new strategies of the Information Age will also mean opening big windows of opportunity in the most unlikely and uncomfortable places. Inevitably, innovation will require us to vigorously pursue ethical solutions that disturb the status quo and ask us to rise above the trivial, adversarial, and political trenches of corporate warfare, bureaucracy, and misplaced micromanagement. The future's employment requirements will invite us to look around and question within, to leverage our confidence to amplify our brand and market our skillset. Tomorrow's leaders will be brave enough to scale the dangerous peaks of an increasingly competitive and ethically challenged mountain range. They will drive the problematic conversations that illuminate the valleys in between. To be part of that conversation means stepping outside your comfortable office, sticking your neck out, and adjusting your eyes to the new light.

The building blocks of this first strategy, while familiar to the new disciplines and emerging technologies of the Information Age, have been around in one form or another for centuries. These include planning, audits, analytics, optimization, and quality assurance. That's because most of the preeminent wonders in life take time and precision to build, as evidenced by their remnants and legacy. And that means opportunity. Take King Solomon's temple. It wasn't built on the fly. The architect Hiram had thousands of apprentices, fellows, and master stonemasons he relied on to ensure his project management plan didn't fail. Each of those workers benefited to some degree from the master's plan. There was a lot of precious time spent on the details and responsibilities delegated to others. It's the same with all of the modern marvels today, from those that transport us across oceans to those we hold in our very hands. In each of humanity's significant accomplishments, there has always been a wealth of opportunity, achieved through a series of many minor goals, seized on by people just like you. Observation and cadence are crucial to pinpointing those opportunities and seeing that magical forest through the trees.

Broken down jalopies

The *Gaps are Opportunities* strategy is rooted in a meditation on the importance of listening and observation and proves in short order wherever we look, especially in the weakest areas of a business, that there is always room for optimization. Those employees who seize upon and fix gaps in areas like production, risk, or quality assurance often become the most valuable players on the grid. They grow into the leaders that management loves to promote. Gaps and deficiencies in an existing program, a product, or a team can be the very best opportunities available to make your mark. History is chock-full of stories where a man or woman came along and "re-invented" a part of a wheel.

One of the most amusing success stories exemplifying this point comes from the first part of the twentieth century. It involves a weary soldier returning from World War I. As the story goes, the GI was tired but also thrilled to be alive after countless friends had been killed, and so much of the world he knew destroyed. He was discharged in California and put on a Pullman train packed with other vets traveling from San Francisco to the East Coast. Like his fellow soldiers, the young man enjoyed his share of spirits in the bar car, and by the time they crossed over into New Mexico, most of the train's passengers were quite drunk. Naturally, overconsumption can lead to brawling, and that's what occurred by early noon. He held his own for a while, but eventually, he was thrown from the caboose about 15 miles outside of Albuquerque. In those days, that was the middle of nowhere.

If that wasn't bad enough, he only had enough money to buy himself a bus ticket to finish the last leg of the trip and maybe half a sandwich. Slightly drunk and out of luck, he began walking down the road parallel to the railroad towards town. As he sobered up along the path, he started noticing a lot of broken-down sedans, pickup trucks, and roadsters abandoned along the highway, likely having run out of gas. Remember, this was 1918, before GPS and call boxes, let alone gas stations... in the desert! Well, this young man thought a lot about those beat-up clunkers, and in between each one, as he made his way to civilization, he began thinking about what the vehicles represented. By the time he finally made it to town, he had come up with one hell of an idea.

Despite being parched and stinking to high heaven, he abandoned his plans to purchase a bus ticket and used what was left in his pocket to put a payment down on a tow truck. The next day he filled up the tank and set back along that road he'd traversed the afternoon before. Well, wouldn't you know it? He picked up every darn one of those lonely jalopies and dragged them back to a lot he'd rented from the same lessor who extended him credit for the tow truck.

Less than a decade later that GI was the third-largest scrap metal salesman in the Southwest United States. By the time he died, about the richest man in Albuquerque. He never quite made it home to Boston, but he did learn first-hand about how your journey is often more enjoyable, and profitable than arriving at your destination.

So, what are your broken-down jalopies? What are the business processes, products, or teams you see broken down and in need of repair or improvement around your organization or community? How can you, like that GI, turn a real crap situation into one that benefits not just you, but ultimately the world around you? Can you identify the gaps in between the stops along the way to your goals? Are you ready to seize the day? Are you thrilled to be alive like that weary soldier the day he was thrown from the train?

You indeed can find and fill the gaps with a growth mindset that sees the positive in the negative, that builds from the ashes, that polishes and reinvents both tried and true and also invents the brand new. Are you in a highly regulated industry or a business that's dependent on rules and best practices governing things like AI and Big Data? If so consider:

- **Finding:** high-priority compliance, legal or technical automation processes in need
- **Identifying:** a toolset or strategy that is efficient and defensible, or a team that can turn around a ship
- **Marketing:** cost and risk mitigation benefits to your business partners and stakeholders

For some, that agenda might be too much work. But with that attitude, good luck getting called on to right the ship. After all, a bad attitude is like a flat tire. And as an old man I know from

Albuquerque would tell you, you can't get darn near anywhere with one of those.

Optics: perception becomes reality

These days everybody wants to be perceived as a "thought leader" and "focused on strategy." That's a reasonable and legitimate goal. But strategy must be complemented by subject matter expertise, and too generalized of a strategy is frequently where our most painful productivity issues originate. Sooner or later, somebody has to roll up their sleeves, become the specialist, or take responsibility for coordinating a team's collective thoughts into a coherent game plan. It's no surprise that most generalists begin their careers as specialists.

It's the substantive work that ultimately refines your capabilities and gives you the insight to lead big projects and teams. I'll leave the specific number of hours required for expertise to Malcolm Gladwell. But the truth remains that the only way you gain experience is by taking on the dirty work and assuming ownership over both success and failure. What matters to management as much as the outcome is how you are perceived while responding to those challenges and how you carry yourself through the ups and downs. How you handle the *blows* matters more than how you take the *bows*.

We're all aware that certain projects, those in which repetitive, mundane, administrative, or technical work is required, are avoided like the plague by line employees and management alike. It's not as exciting as "What should we do next with this ridiculous budget or patented technology?!" When a project does happen to spark immediate interest and quickly garner executive support, once it moves past the planning stages, it too can begin to feel like nobody on the team wants to be bothered with the specific logistics. It ends up either a shell of itself, on the chopping block, or just the back burner. This is especially true in larger organizations where the majority of stakeholders are not incentivized to profit from the idea or initiative's success directly.

Surprisingly, what can blossom from these hellish projects are new, bold leaders, since these are also opportunities for individuals willing to board the ship and chart the obstacle course. These are the champions in life and work who drive initiatives forward because they're more interested in accomplishing something and learning new skills than getting (or stealing) the credit. They are playing a long game, and that's how they outwit those who would short their own stock. Of course, we all know individuals who have been elevated by less ethical means and have gone on to lead companies, even governments! But there is no long-term professional value for lifetime purveyors of immediate gratification.

Modern knowledge workers expect to graduate into advanced roles and focus increasingly on delegation. Yet a strictly hands-off attitude ultimately results in us easily falling out of touch with basic business operations, over time making us seem unrelatable and aloof to our co-workers and customers. We naively assume technology or corporate bureaucracy will shoulder all the tedious processes we're tasked with rather than striving to understand its impact on our businesses and identifying room for further efficiency.

Masses of employees, especially those basking in the spend-it-or-lose-it public sector, have grown comfortable with management throwing money at a problem or bringing in consultants to clean up a mess instead of tackling causation. As leaders and executives, we never want to take a step backward and be viewed as unwilling to trust and delegate. Yet there is much to be said for staying familiar with, remaining involved in, and practicing the discipline in which you claim to have expertise.

In this Information Age, we need to stay current with the problems our industry is facing, intimately, so that our ideas remain fresh, so we can retool and modernize the principles that have worked for us. Those principles and optics help get our teams to score on goal posts that always seem to be moving.

The worst they can say is no

If my 88-year-old mother ever had a LinkedIn profile, her headline would read something like "Former ingenue, entrepreneur, dreamer, and the rest is none of your business, my dear." But to those who've had the privilege to know her over the decades, her mantra has always been, quite emphatically, to treat everybody with dignity. That was one of the main reasons she was receptive to opportunity.

She began working from an early age and later helped my father through chiropractic school by working long hours as a Hollywood extra during the fifties and sixties. Though never seeking stardom, she knocked on enough doors to get a lot of good work, saved some seed money, and established relationships that would eventually transform her life. Mom leveraged her positive attitude and tough shell to find opportunities, sell her strengths, and laugh off rejection. "It's no big deal," she always told me as a kid when the chips were down and she says the same thing to me now.

Most importantly, and by example, Mom taught me that you should never feel afraid to negotiate a deal because the absolute worst "they," a client, customer, or possible employer can say is... no.

Seven windows of opportunity

In the next seven chapters, we demonstrate how these lessons frame windows of opportunity opening up in fields like blockchain, big data, IoT, and artificial intelligence. We begin with a journey to Zambia to learn how distributed ledger technology is empowering impoverished communities to demand visibility into supply chains and realize their potential. Next, a renowned data scientist lays out some of the ethical challenges that AI has left on our doorstep. Then we teleport to the Netherlands, where we discover the strategy behind how information flows in the international court system. We then zip back to the US to prepare for a data tsunami with a leading IoT software developer. With that knowledge under our belt, we make our way to California and sit down with a smart city CIO to see how new technologies are impacting the public. We pick up from there and take an autonomous drive with a telematics specialist from America's largest insurer, before finally heading back to Africa to witness opportunity in action. We'll see you there!

Chapter 1

Blockchain for Common Good

Ashish Gadnis, Founder and CEO, BanQu
Topics: Blockchain, Logistics, Upward Mobility

"Old economic models have failed because they look at the ability to help people out of poverty separate from enabling people in poverty to take part in the supply chain."
Ashish Gadnis

Ashish Gadnis is Chief Executive Officer of BanQu and a recognized thought leader in the burgeoning blockchain community. He chairs the Financial Inclusion Working Committee for the Wall Street Blockchain Alliance and travels the world, explaining how this revolutionary new technology is transforming the way we contemplate supply chain economics. He holds an MBA from the University of Minnesota's Carlson School of Management and graduated from the Global Leadership and Public Policy program at the Harvard Kennedy School of Government.

Q: Ashish, we first learned about your life's work at a conference exploring how technology impacts the human condition. You shared the story of selling your firm, Forward Hindsight, and soon after founding BanQu to fight extreme poverty by leveraging blockchain. How did you choose this path?

A: It was a means to an end. I was born and raised in a slum in India 50 years ago. And I grew up hating being poor. Pretty much all my life growing up, I was poor. When I moved to the US and started building my life, and got my own deal and started building Forward Hindsight, I always asked myself, "If somebody will buy this thing, and if it all works out, I could walk away and try to help address the extreme poverty situation in the world." So, it wasn't exactly like other entrepreneurs who have that itch to do the next big thing.

For me, it was pretty organized. I sold my company, and I just started volunteering in the Congo for a couple of years and then had some experiences that forced me to reflect even further. That's when I realized I could volunteer for the rest of my life, or I could actually start something like BanQu and make a dent in the universe. So, the selling of my company was just a means to my end. I knew my calling was around the corner, so I sold it and ultimately just walked away.

Q: With BanQu, people ensure their economic identity with an immutable record of their transactions in a system benefiting the entire supply chain. How does the company go about realizing those goals?

A: Over the last two and a half years, we've determined that 2.7 billion people, including refugees displaced and those in extreme poverty zones, participate in some sort of a supply chain. That can mean you're the most impoverished farmer in Congo growing coffee, cacao, or shea butter, you know, the ingredients that go into cosmetics, and your contributions show up in brands like eight dollar lattes and expensive body lotions. And in examining their participation, we realized that current models for getting people out of poverty have failed.

Old economic models have failed because they look at the ability to help people out of poverty separate from *enabling* people in poverty to take part in the supply chain. We took another route. Nobody had ever done it. We said, "What if the people who are absolutely in that last mile get to participate equally?" Then the value for the brand is suddenly more relevant.

Let's use a simple example. If you're buying cacao in Ghana and you're a large chocolate company, there's a good chance today that your last mile farmers are extremely poor and also invisible. No matter how much traceability, transparency, or fair trade you implement, until and unless that farmer can participate in his data, to know, for example, "I'm selling 40 kilos every other week to this big brand," then that farmer will continue to live in poverty. That poor farmer today has everything stacked against him or her, especially if conditions are rough.

I was just in Zambia a week and a half ago, and I saw a first-hand example of this problem, which was that women farmers have to borrow at a higher price point. Women farmers are often finding themselves on the short end of the stick because they're not able, in a multitude of cases, to prove their history. What happens if she is selling 40 kilos upstream, and there are seven middlemen? After she sells her coffee, somebody picks it up, then brings it to somebody else, the next one goes to the warehouse, and eventually she's lost the ability to track her product. You see, while the internet has come to people in poverty, it hasn't actually pulled people out of extreme poverty, let alone permanently. There's mobile money, there's big data, AI, etc., but none of those models have ever allowed that mother, that farmer, to participate equally.

When I say participate equally, it's very basic. To me, participate equally means that one, she has a physical, digitally stored copy of that transaction that nobody can ever steal or manipulate. Two, she can prove her transaction history, which legitimizes her existence in that supply chain. Three, it allows her to now leverage that data in a way that reduces her cost of borrowing. It allows her to be portable. That's how we decided to look at blockchain. Nobody has ever done this. People keep talking about how they're going to use blockchain for good, but we're one of the only ones doing it every day, taking a commercial approach while being simultaneously profoundly purpose-driven.

We started a for-profit, for-purpose software company, and now the largest brands are coming to us because it solves two sides of the problem for them. One side is that the supply chain now becomes more cost-effective and efficient. They get better visibility into the supply chain in terms of quality, market access, and forecasting, which enables an ecosystem for crop insurance, climate protection, education. The other side of the coin is that they can start addressing issues like gender equality and labor rights.

Q: *In your model, BanQu offers a software-as-a-service software (SaaS) platform that supports six key United Nations Sustainable Development Goals (UN-SDGs) out-of-the-box. Together, this "Economic Identity Passport" is used by corporations, governments, and International Non-Government Organizations (INGO's) looking to meet their UN-SDG goals and other commitments. Since launching, what have you found are the most utilized of the tools?*

A: They're intertwined. This is why we took a platform approach and why it's software as a service. A lot of companies are going to focus on water, healthcare, or gender. We looked at these six UN-SDG's and realized that they should always be looked at together. Let's look at an example. We're live in eight countries. As I mentioned, I was recently in one in Sub-Saharan Africa, and we're talking the bottom of the pyramid. No running water, no sanitation, no paved roads, high malnutrition. Tough as it gets. Yet their farmers (especially the women) are knowledgeable and resilient, and they grow crops because there is a market. BanQu gives them confidence and dignity because their harvest can be sold with full traceability and transparency. At the end of the day, it's a circular economy, and now the woman farmer has an economic identity.

Q: *Can you explain that concept, economic identity, in detail?*

A: For us, economic identity is the ability to prove our identity in those types of transactions. So, if I sold you 40 kilos every three weeks, you pay me money for the quality and the quantity, and now it's history. But one aspect of identity alone is useless. If you just show up at a bank and say, "Hey, I'm so-and-so, this is my driver's license, and you should give me a good interest rate on a car loan" Well, they're going to ask you to take a hike. Whereas if you showed up with your social security card and your education, you're taken seriously. It's just the way the world works. If I know a little more about you, I'm going to treat you with a bit more dignity, and that's what our solution supports.

Q: For organizations applying this private blockchain solution, are there some modules or some components more useful than others in the immediate term?

A: The most pressing one is the supply chain connection. For example, some of the largest brands in the food business will sign up with us for immediate traceability and transparency into their existing crop flows. Just like they're buying Salesforce.com or Oracle or SAP. They subscribe to our platform. We configure for things like language, currency, workflow, asset classes. We also have a meta-data framework that our clients can now create themselves for KPIs and metrics in real-time. We go live, and it gets deployed to the farmer who doesn't have a smartphone, just via SMS, and now the last mile is connected in real-time. Traceable, transparent, and the farmer participates equally.

So, when a transaction happens, they bring a bag of cacao or coffee or whatever to market, you, as the farmer get an SMS message confirming the transaction, and the location and an authentication token. We don't mess with cryptocurrencies. We use pure blockchain. Now you have a copy that says you dropped off 40 kilos, plus here's the quality, plus here's the payout and it's secured and private.

The key empowering impact is that you have permanent digital proof of that asset from tree-to-cup or mine-to-battery. As the transaction progresses, you have a record of the payout, which is a big deal in emerging markets, especially around security and in terms of building your credibility in that crop flow. If you were dropping 40 kilos every two weeks and a broker was taking it off of your hands, you cannot prove that you have been growing a good crop. So, as the weeks go by, now the farmer can see her entire history, and it's validated in the ledger, which makes her bankable. It benefits both the brand and the farmer as well as the entire supply chain.

Q: Have you begun to tap the big data aspect of it? If so, what challenges will that bring in terms of our evolving regulatory climate?

A: Yes and No. We have an open API, and that lets banks, mobile operators, and others integrate with BanQu. Also, we integrate with backend accounting systems, ERP's, inventory management, record-keeping systems, and so forth. So, when these steps are happening, clients are already starting to do their analysis because they can say, hey, we're starting to see a good quality crop in this region. We've had cases where the fraud detection piece, because of blockchain, is already showing results because everybody entering the supply chain is known and wants to be known. Everybody is now getting a copy of the transaction they participate in and its improving transparency.

From a data analytics perspective, the big brands like us because now it gives them the visibility into their last mile that they never had. Especially from a cash flow perspective, from a standpoint of trying to reduce fluctuation around receivables, supply chain insurance, and production planning. In a lot of these markets, it's all cash-based and manual 90-day reconciliation process to complete.

Having said all that, we don't own anybody's data, which is a key piece. We will never own anybody's data because that would then defeat the purpose of creating a blockchain application. So, the data ownership is with the brand in terms of the transactions that they are participating in, but the data ownership is also with the farmer or the homeless person or the refugees. They now have a copy of their data that they can use.

The way we built it, the end-user can now prove their existence or the right to be forgotten. So, we have this permission-based ledger where the farmer can say, "I want to be able to show a bank my data." And he can give permission to the bank. Or she could say, "I don't want to participate anymore, and I have the right to go dark." Because at the end of the day, that last mile farmer in BanQu has the ability to own, access, monetize, and permission their data. So, the analytics applies but not at the last mile.

Q: One of the goals in conducting these interviews is gaining a better understanding of the evolving role of data and its impact on society and governance. You've lived and worked with people on all levels of the pyramid. What role is blockchain playing here?

A: Occasionally, people push back on the work we do and say, you know, farmers aren't literate. And I take offense to that because I've never met a farmer or any person in poverty who said, "Don't tell me how much crop or garments or diamonds I sold you," or "don't tell me the price or confirmation of the payout." So actually farmers, miners, garment workers, they're very literate and brilliant. Here's the data issue there. And it has a big implication for governance. In my past life, I worked in Sarbanes-Oxley, in compliance and audit, on segregation of duties. I was deep into the compliance framework and familiar with all those kinds of issues. In the example of the farmer I've given, what happens is that the world takes for granted that the farmer's data rights don't exist. The rights for poor women that are growing your coffee are compromised every day. We took a different approach and found that distributed ledger blockchain technology empowers the poorest while strengthening the largest global brands.

If you decouple the currency side, blockchain is immutability, consensus. Currency is currency. The real value is consensus and immutability. And that's where a lot of people miss the true value of blockchain. We took an approach saying the farmer, the slave labor that's making the jeans, and also the refugee, should have bleed control over all the data that he or she is either forced to participate or is willing to participate in. And that has kind of solved part of the confusion around the General Data Protection Requirement and data privacy because at the end of the day, if you implement it the right way, which we've proven in the last 18 months, the farmer owns their data, right?

So, if the farmer is selling to the coffee company, but the coffee company says, "Hey, I don't want to buy your coffee from now on," in today's world, that coffee company is just going to walk away with all this amazing data on the farmer. That's the way the world works today. Yet if you use blockchain, yes, the farmer and the coffee company relationship changes. The company walks away with all this data, but the farmer now has a copy of the data that nobody can ever take away. That's how we implement it. And that's why we're upfront. BanQu doesn't own anybody's data. And at the end of the day, if my bank customer goes away, in my last mile, because we have a B to B to C model, the customer never loses access to that data because we have the proper safeguards.

Q: This all seems like the ideal career track for those who want to use their education to advance a good cause. What is your advice for a young person just starting their journey? How do they even begin to think about getting into something like blockchain?

A: For one, you'll probably have to fail a million times. That's the easiest answer. But from a career standpoint, I would definitely get into computer science or some technology stack. The big five – the internet of things, blockchain, big data, artificial and quantum computing. Those five technologies will transform every aspect of our lives, good or bad. If you want to start the next charity or the next big thing, you'd better be knowledgeable about these areas because although you might end up being a brain surgeon, you're still probably going to need to understand one of these five. That would be number one.

Number two would be just jump in, get a good startup going, and be willing to fail. Only have an expectation that you'll fail. A lot of young people make the mistake of joining a large company just for a safety net or join a startup because they want to make a million dollars overnight. Both of those motivations can result in the wrong approaches to success, in my mind.

In my opinion, if you're in your 20's until you're 35, you've got to say, "I'm going to live in eight different countries, fail 15 different times and be completely broke." But then, after that, you might just have a much better chance of hitting it big.

Chapter 2

Ethical Underpinnings of Artificial Intelligence

Dr. Anand Rao, Global AI Lead, PricewaterhouseCoopers
Topics: Artificial Intelligence, Big Data, Ethics

"Deep learning is not equal to deep understanding. I think we must go beyond it and look at all other forms of learning and intelligence."
Dr. Anand Rao

Dr. Anand Rao, Ph.D., MBA, MSc, is the Global Artificial Intelligence Lead at PricewaterhouseCoopers. He has over 30 years of experience in behavioral economics, risk management, and statistical and computational analytics. He has co-edited four books, published over 50 peer-reviewed papers, and previously served as the Program Director for the Center for Intelligent Decision Systems at the University of Melbourne. Dr. Rao received his Ph.D. in finance technology from Melbourne University, his master's from the University of Sydney, and his MSc in computer science from the Birla Institute of Science and Technology.

Q: Dr. Rao, how has the relationship between academic institutions and the business world evolved in the era of big data and analytics? Is it a balanced symbiotic relationship, and what are its benefits for startups and students alike?

A: If you're talking about the AI and big data world, one of the challenges that academics have in this area is that they've always tended to have the thought leadership role and control over the publications and so forth, but they haven't had the data.

Businesses have the data, large volumes of consumer-level data. So, the data is one element.

Also, over the past few years, we've seen the need for considerable computing power, which again tends to be less available on the university-side these days and more in the business sector. Business sectors are running large machines with powerful GPUs, quantum computing, all of which is quite expensive for academics to support. That's been one of the challenges in terms of their research.

In fact, in the big data world, in the AI world, the academics are lagging, and additional levels of investment are needed. In the good old days, there were all these joint efforts in supercomputing, and governments were investing very heavily. Since then, at least over the past couple of decades, most of that funding has pretty much vanished. That type of investment is the same one universities are now asking of businesses. Of course, where the relationship is good, there exist productive symbiotic relationships. Where the companies can provide the data, the academics can provide both the techniques and the people, basically university students, postdocs, to analyze that data.

Q: *The Futurist Roy Amara famously noted, "We tend to overestimate the effect of a technology in the short run and underestimate the effect in the long run." Within the context of the digital disruptions of the last few decades, do you believe his statement still holds up, or do we have a better grasp of where technology is taking us?*

A: In the case of AI, mainly, it's still very much true. As we know, there is quite a lot of hype around it with everyone saying, "Hey, AI is going to take over. We're going to lose all our jobs," which I think, at least in the near term, is not going to happen. There are still many hurdles that need to be overcome, so I don't think all of that fear is warranted. In the longer term, yes. There is a slow progression of value being added by these machines.

So, humans need to position themselves in vocations that are value-add, as opposed to repetitive tasks.

Those roles are where most of the automation is happening. I think everyone needs to ask themselves the question, "If I'm doing something very repetitive or manual, am I adding value here?" So, that's the key. Because more and more of those responsibilities will be taken over by the machine. At the moment, people shouldn't be worried, but in the longer term, certainly, AI will undoubtedly completely transform the job market.

Q: You've spoken quite passionately on the ethics of emerging technologies. At a recent World Economic Forum meeting, you remarked how AI is a force for good but warned that there remains a lot of fear and misconceptions preventing adoption. What are today's most problematic ethical obstacles for developers, and how are they overcoming them?

A: The foremost ethical challenge is the notion of bias and fairness. There are a lot of ethical principles, and we're all told we should treat every person the same and not be biased either by gender, ethnicity, views, age, all of the different criteria. So, we can say that. But if I'm a data scientist, the question becomes, how do I make sure that I'm not introducing any bias in the way my algorithm is making recommendations? If I am working at a bank and I'm writing a machine learning algorithm that decides the credit limits for individuals, how exactly do I go about doing that? How do I make sure that what I'm doing is not unfair by any scheme of things? There are several instances like that in every industry.

The reason it's so problematic is that we use historical data for machine learning, and when you use historical data, as in any society, it may be biased in one way or the other, right? Either to specific ethnic groups or genders, and that can all get reflected in the AI recommendation. There have been some very well-known cases, one very recently involving two large players, one tech player and another, a bank. In this example, the male goes in and applies for a payment card, and he'll get a certain credit limit. But in the case of the spouse, even in a joint account, if the wife applies for the same card, the credit limit is somehow much lower. The question suddenly becomes, why? These stories are now finding their way into the press, and so there's a lot of discussions to be had around issues of bias.

There are, by some accounts, 32 definitions of fairness. For data scientists, do they even have the time to understand all the implications of each of them on what they're building? That's an enormous challenge. Another challenge is, plainly, "How do I explain what my algorithm is doing?" It's a tall order for certain types of techniques within AI.

Another big issue is safety. Is the AI that I'm building safe? Is it tested under all kinds of extreme conditions? The more sophisticated the system, the tougher it is to test some of these things. So, those represent challenges from an ethical perspective, even though there's no doubt as to what the ethics are to a large extent. So, while people agree that AI should be safe, it should be explainable. It should be fair. How exactly to do it is by no means close to being solved.

Q: One impact of the adoption of AI is the prospect that companies will need fewer employees to reach or surpass their goals. You've said the top three industries ripe for disruption include finance, healthcare, and auto. To what degree will the workforce in those industries be displaced over the next 15 years?

A: We should look at it, not necessarily as the displacement, but as an augmentation or a change in the job. Yes, there will be a certain number of people who will be displaced, but a majority of them will likely see their job description change. I think, like the previous revolutions that have occurred, AI will ultimately create more jobs, different types of them, which may not even be attributed to a specific AI solution. I don't see mass-scale unemployment where machines will replace everything. I don't see that situation coming at all. I expect that people will need to become more comfortable using machines, using recommendations and learning when to use judgment. Deciding, "When do I accept the machine's recommendation versus when do I go on my intuition and experience?" For example, just because my personalized book-recommender suggests a particular collection doesn't mean I'm buying each and every book. Right? I use my judgment, read through my options, and then decide. Irrespective of what the system says, I'm still making certain decisions. Over time, using discretion and AI, we'll get better at what we're doing.

One of the concepts we use "man-plus-machine" is better than just "either one on their own." So, in spite of all the machine intelligence, just using a machine isn't the right thing yet for a multitude of serious decisions that we make. By the same token, just using humans without having some machine aid, in numerous cases, is also not optimal. That's why the man-plus-the-machine is a better way of approaching it right now.

Q: *What or who initially influenced you to pursue a career in data science?*

A: I found my way into AI way back in 1985. I did my Ph.D. at that time, completed my computer science degree, and the only thing I could think of was wanting to get into AI. I was just fascinated by the human thinking process and being able to mimic that in a machine.

Q: *What sage advice might you have for those drawn to AI domains like machine learning, robotics, and neural networks? How do they break-in to an industry that seems so daunting and sophisticated?*

A: I guess for the AI data scientists, the first advice I would give is deep learning is not the same as deep understanding. And I know there's a lot of excitement around deep learning, but I think we must go beyond it and look at all other forms of learning and intelligence. The way deep learning traditionally works is based on what patterns you can draw from the data. That's just one way that we learn, and we also learn in other ways. And not enough work is being done in other ways of learning. So, continuous learning. Learning at the symbolic level. Learning not just from patterns, but by inference. I'm sure that at the highest level, even some of the leading researchers of deep learning are very conscious of some of the drawbacks, and are trying to address that. Also, as an AI scientist, you need to be open-minded in embracing different things, to be able to move forward in the creation of AI. So, that would be one piece of advice.

For someone wanting to break into the industry, from a business point of view, there are some easy things that you can do with AI to give you or your business a big return on investment and lead to career growth. We call it using "cool" AI to solve boring problems. What I mean by boring problems is the back office. With most businesses, there's a lot of invoices, and there's a lot of text documents. People are just going through them, extracting information. That's a very tedious task or a boring task if you like. AI can help a lot in those areas. It can remove all the drudgery. There is a lot of it left in the service economy as well that AI professionals can help remove. Of course, removing that drudgery means you then need to start adding value, rather than just replacing mechanical tasks. But, once you accept that challenge, I think there are indefinite opportunities to start doing more exciting things in the space.

Chapter 3

Directing the Flow of Information

Dr. Jones Lukose Ongalo, Information Management Officer, International Criminal Court
Topics: Data Governance

"We now live in a world where small sets of information can alter the economies of the most powerful organizations and states on the planet. It is a world where compact streams of sensitive information can digitally leak and cause violent reactions from people living far and beyond the source."
Dr. Jones Lukose Ongalo

Dr. Jones Lukose Ongalo, MBA, Ph.D., is the Information Management Officer for the Court Pénale Internationale at the Criminal Court in the Hague. He has spent the last two decades developing and implementing strategies to achieve operational effectiveness and regulatory compliance for engineering firms in energy and utility sectors and judicial organizations within Africa, Europe, and the Americas. Jones received his MBA from Hague University and his Ph.D. in Computer Science from Heriot-Watt University.

Q: Dr. Ongalo, your work, and research have taken you to the four corners of the world, including Kenya, Rwanda, Botswana, Jamaica, the UK, and now the Netherlands. It's there you presently direct an enterprise-wide information program for the International Criminal Court. What is the most ubiquitous challenge you've encountered across so many diverse cultures, and how has it shaped how you think about solutions for international entities?

A: I've worked in organizations where data is everywhere,

but no one is directing its flow. There is a lot of information collected and stored that simply does not fit within the organization's strategy. The organization may claim that it is going in a particular direction, but the data it holds does not provide the required evidence or proof. That experience has led me to reconsider my role in the organization. In such environments, it is my first priority to help determine the real purpose and value of data to the organization. In other words, lend a hand in crafting the strategy of the organization by leveraging information management principles.

Those principles recognize that we now live in a world where small sets of information can alter the economies of the most powerful organizations and states on the planet. It is a world where compact streams of sensitive information can digitally leak and cause violent reactions from people living far and beyond the source. Tiny words or images transported via exotic technology can lead to wide-spread panic across whole populations, even wars. A world where information is fragmented, infinitely raising an infinite number of world views and identities. It is a world where the same information is interpreted differently in space and time. It is a world where information is presented in constant flux, with the only constant being surprise.

Whatever your personal or political convictions might be, I challenge you to consider new ways of looking at information management. It won't help to retreat to our old maps and models because the more we do that, the more frustrated we become. We need new techniques to navigate the chaos, filter the wrong, and point us to the significant. The new information manager will thrive and even love to embrace the chaos of information by applying new lenses and insights. He or she should be ready to be inspired to experiment and try out new ideas and solutions.

Perhaps the information manager of today believes they need to invest in uncommon skills such as engineering, mathematics, and statistics to remain relevant. But core values are still more important to performance and outcomes. It is now very possible to visualize the behavior of information management teams and predict their performance using tools that align and measure core values to information management practices. Close examinations of the way employees handle information flowing in the organization directly reflect how core values such as respect, transparency, accountability, and integrity positively influence productivity. A value-based approach is, therefore, very effective in establishing healthy information management practices that can endure the test of time.

Q: In your roles as both consultant and practitioner, your focus has been on advising public entities, whether they be utilities or court systems. How are you deploying the new discipline of information governance in these organizations to support business objectives?

A: To start, information governance needs to be much more than a formal system of internal tasks and reporting relationships or something that occasionally shows up on intranet sites and bulletin boards. Information management leaders understand that governance schemes must be carefully matched to the organization's purpose and environment. Good governance also creates links between authority, responsibility, accountability, and an organization's actual data.

Information governance influences behavior and helps shape an organization's culture over time, much like a skeleton gives shape to the body and allows stability in motion. This dimension guides the practitioner in understanding how to use information as an enabler of change judiciously and how it can be aligned appropriately to nurture effective behavior and reporting relationships.

I seek these types of principles and use them as values to transcend technology, methodologies, and techniques. Without principles, sensitive information is mishandled, individuals lose their way, and organizational anxiety ensues. This creates confusion, conflicts, paralysis, and cannibalization of energy. As part of my leadership strategy, I set clear principles and manage these proactively rather than in damage control when a crisis occurs. I am mindful of how I handle information within the organization and try to inspire other staff to be so as well through that behavior.

Q: How do you determine your information program's priorities?

A: Surprisingly, some priorities are not arrived at rationally but via experience and intuition. In the modern approach, the information manager needs to assume that in complex systems, prediction and prioritization are nearly impossible; the information manager accepts greater indeterminacy and ambiguity. In light of this, the modern information manager needs to rely on intuitive feel for situations, and trusts in the character, creativity, and abilities that they and others bring to the profession. It is essentially a "dance" but created by "jazz artists" that intuitively trust in each other's abilities and skills to produce something of higher value than the sum of their individual talents.

Q: The International Criminal Court has a dynamic public-facing portal where voluminous and sensitive court documents are indexed, redacted, and made searchable for the public once authorized. How has this robust tool affected people's interactions with the court, and has it helped raise awareness about its mission?

A: Yes, the court recognized that it needed to adapt its online presence, ensuring that modernization reflected its status as a top judicial organization. This view was widely supported by staff and external stakeholders consulted before the start of the project. The digital environment of the Court is continuously evolving, and with it the way it does business online and expectations of end-users. In particular, progress needs to be rapid for social networking and mobile access. A wide-ranging and sustained transformation of the Court's web presence was initiated, encompassing the tools used, how the Court presented itself to and engaged with all audiences, and how this information was managed and monitored.

The initial development phase utilized a different philosophy and approach to our web presence. The result was a simplified and focused presentation of court content. However, later transformations grew more challenging, given increasing volumes of information and the degree of customization necessary to support existing services and teams.

Q: The entire information management community before 1983, when ARPANET was born, consisted of a relatively small group of librarians, archivists, and museum curators around the world. In just a few decades, the internet has fundamentally altered the way we access, catalog, and contextualize facts and ultimately process knowledge. Ensuring context and narrative is no longer the role of a Putman editor or an associated press. Has this "democratization of data" impacted our ability as a society to discern truth, when truth and the very integrity of records can be so easily manipulated for political, personal, or other nefarious reasons?

A: The notion of all of us information managers becoming a part of the data-information system, as seen in modern (digital) networks today, is not entirely new. Today, the information manager is no longer external and neutral, but through the act of ingestion and dissemination becomes a part of the information ecosystem. It also has enormous implications on the role and responsibilities of information managers in the born-digital world.

The quandary is that the process of accountability is entangled in complexity. As information managers come to understand more about democratized data, it seems increasingly likely that events on a data level are not only unpredictable but simply infinitely more complex than ever previously imagined. The actions on data in one location often have a remarkable and unexpected impact on another seemingly disconnected group of data. Because of this, one key facet of information accountability recognizes that every action can have unforeseen and exotic consequences. In practice, this means that the outcome of any given policy decision or action is nowhere near as predictable as previously supposed: ensuring protection from viruses does not necessarily bring security, policies intended to manage protection can create crises in other areas, such as data integrity and provenance.

To deal with this data dilemma, I would propose that information managers develop the ability to see the whole, to see beyond their immediate repository. Just as relationships between tiny data packets are symmetrically balanced, so the relationship between information managers and data sources should be meticulously balanced, with neither side holding too much power over the other.

Chapter 4

Establishing a Framework to Sustain the IoT Tsunami

Priya Keshav, Founder and CEO, Meru Data
Topics: Internet of Things, Compliance

"Companies need to recognize that we are at an inflection point in terms of IoT and data and begin to reframe their overarching governance strategies."
Priya Keshav

Priya Keshav is the founder and CEO of Meru Data, a software company that provides corporate information governance solutions. Before developing her own patented products, she led KPMG's Forensic Technology Services Practice in the Southwest United States. She graduated from the Warrington College of Business Administration and received her MBA from the University of Florida.

Q: Priya, you've written extensively regarding complex ethical issues born out of the mostly unregulated Internet of Things (IoT) industry. Is there a universal awareness of IoT's potential risks yet or even an understanding of how to begin addressing its challenges?

A: I think there is universal recognition that the use of IoT is certainly introducing novel challenges and ethical questions. However, I would not consider there is universal awareness or understanding of its risks at this point. The use and adoption of IoT are rapidly increasing, the solutions being developed are integrating multiple industries, and yet we are just scratching the surface of what is possible. So, I think we are at a point today where we recognize those challenges are going to arise, but I do not believe we have fully understood the nature nor extent of them.

Industry players and regulators are likely at the same crossroads and thinking about appropriate frameworks for addressing possibilities and threats. I don't believe regulatory pressures from either Europe or the US are yet the primary drivers for the growing awareness. But yes, there are regulatory interests that have the industry taking notice. However, there are very few specific regulations, such as California bill SB327, which deal with information privacy and connected IoT devices. Regulatory efforts around IoT have been guideline focused, and agencies like the Consumer Products Safety Commission and the Federal Trade Commission are getting involved.

Q: With your Meru Data platform, you've strived to develop a workflow and reporting tool that manages data governance for clients based on best practices as opposed to specific regulatory directives. Is that strategy feasible given the often rigid, prescriptive requirements in rules like the General Data Protection Requirement (GDPR)?

A: Yes, because at Meru, we have focused on developing software that can sustain data governance programs. That's the reason we have taken a fundamental approach to creating solutions that are not solely aimed at specific regulatory initiatives. It would be harder to maintain tools that are focused on just addressing a few specific regulations. We believe it makes more sense to ensure instead that the organization can harness data as an asset effectively. We think with effective governance in place, complying with regulations becomes easier by design and doesn't place additional technical burdens on organizations.

Internalizing strategic objectives helps companies prepare and respond to the varying rules over the long run. That's why our products are designed to help to develop and maintain, for example, an evergreen data map within the organization. We also help our customers ensure that a long-term plan for managing data remains their focus even as various shorter-term efforts, for example, exercises around data clean-up, are being worked on.

Q: In preparing for the coming "data tsunami," which you called out in a piece for Bloomberg, you advise companies to reexamine their existing compliance frameworks. Do organizations need to rethink their entire strategies as a result of IoT, or do they need to tweak existing guidelines and protocols?

A: Well, the data tsunami is already here, with about 2.5 quintillion bytes of data created every day. This includes types of information that come under the purview of consumer data privacy regulations that are present today. However, this tsunami is going to pale in comparison with the types of information and volumes of data that will get generated by future IoT devices. As IoT devices become ubiquitous in consumers' lives, our current problems with data will almost seem trivial by comparison. Companies need to recognize that we are at an inflection point in terms of IoT and data and begin to reframe their overarching governance strategies. Companies that don't do this will be at a competitive disadvantage, unable to use their data as an asset, and in a constant struggle to keep up with regulatory pressures on how consumer data is safeguarded.

How and whether organizations need to rethink their existing guidelines and protocols depends, of course, on where organizations are today. There is a broad spectrum of information governance program maturity across different organizations. While some companies understand the importance of IG and are well on their way to building a comprehensive IG program, many are still in the initial stages. While most of the companies are doing "something," they are barely scratching the surface when it comes to benefiting from a real information governance program. Almost all organizations are targeting a few of the immediately achievable targets around reducing storage burdens. Most have also realized it is integral to build stakeholder support for their programs to make these sustainable. However, there are still substantial opportunities for companies to position their governance efforts to succeed in an IoT driven future. IoT demands will perhaps provide organizations with the impetus to build their infrastructure with a view towards that future.

Establishing a sound, foundational approach to how the data is created, used, and stored within an organization is primary. With a strong foundation, it isn't necessary to completely rethink the framework to incorporate IoT. The fundamental principles of IG will hold even in an IoT driven world. However, it also important to understand the nature of IoT data, the value it can add to a company, and the challenges it can pose if companies are unprepared. Some of these aspects are discussed in the guidelines and standards I noted, and professionals should keep up with the evolution of these guidelines. For instance, the draft discussion of cybersecurity standards around IoT from the NIST highlights that companies might have to prepare for situations where IoT devices:

- Might not be accessed or monitored like conventional IT assets.
- Can make changes to the physical world and thus can potentially affect human safety or cause damage to equipment and facilities.
- Have differing lifespan expectations and possibly unserviceable hardware.
- Have heterogeneous ownership. Companies might not be able to maintain a complete inventory of all devices and might also have restricted access to the devices.

These issues will make it challenging to have universal recommendations or best practices that can work for all IoT devices. Organizations will need to understand risks based on specific uses of devices and adjust their policies and processes accordingly. Another thing to keep in mind is that managing the security and privacy risks of some of these devices might potentially affect other types of risk or might introduce a new stake in another area. Risks need to be understood and handled holistically.

Q: You spent almost a decade leading one of the best Forensic Technologies Services groups at KPMG. What insights did you learn in that position that have proven helpful in guiding and informing your entrepreneurial ventures?

A: I have seen companies derive marked benefits from being able to steward their data as an asset. If properly done, companies gain tremendous competitive advantages and improve consumer confidence and loyalty. I have also seen how considerable the costs of having to react to regulatory or legal needs for data can be when companies are going through a crisis. Being prepared proactively with better managed IG programs makes a big difference.

I have also seen how IG programs stall if they are manually intensive, or, if it is hard to track progress, or if they do not have stakeholder buy-in. For programs to sustain, there needs to be a clear view of progress and a continuous way to build on successes without ever-increasing efforts. Culturally, I think it is worse to have an IG effort stall than to have no effort at all.

We have tried to build on these documented experiences to provide our customers with sustainable models. This approach has a lot of resonance with companies and has helped us to gain traction with our customers. Enabling companies to position themselves for succeeding in tomorrow's world with even more data has been the other major underpinning of our solutions. In a nutshell, we are trying to make IG sustainable and to encourage and enable companies to develop frameworks that will work today and in the future.

Q: Are there any pearls of wisdom you'd be willing to share that might help a young person or individual thinking about a career in IG, Data Governance, or the IoT? Is it too late to get in on the ground floor on some of these evolving disciplines?

A: No, it is not too late to get involved! There are some extraordinary opportunities to build very successful and satisfying careers in this space. We are at the cusp of massive data-driven changes in most industries. Soon, all kinds of professionals are going to be actively managing new types of data in larger volumes and under evolving regulatory scenarios.

We must realize how our own lives are being altered by IoT every day. Our houses, cars, work, and lives are many times more wired and internet-connected than even a couple of years ago. Locks, doorbell cameras, voice-activated assistants, drones, autopilot cars, smart devices, you name it, it is already happening today. As end-users, we are perfectly positioned to appreciate why this data needs to be managed securely. It's an incredibly in-demand skill to understand the technology generating this data, how companies can derive value from it, and the need to protect and secure it.

Chapter 5

Bridging Strategy and Governance in a Smart City

Kevin Gray, CIO, City of Burbank

Topics: Smart Cities, Business Strategy, Artificial Intelligence

"You have to be a true partner with the business. The technology is the secondary piece. The technology is what you use to try to find the solution for the problem the business is trying to solve."

Kevin Gray

Kevin Gray is the Chief Information Officer for the City of Burbank, leading an IT department responsible for administrative and network management, geographic information systems, and technical services for over 1400 city employees across 15 departments. Before assuming this role, he served as VP of Global Media and IT for Viacom, one of the world's premier entertainment entities, overseeing an international team located across six continents. He received his bachelor's in information systems from California State University, Long Beach, and is a certified Scrum Master and Project Management Professional (PMP).

Q: Kevin, you began your career path at Orion Pictures, administering Unix systems and then directed data center operations for DreamWorks. How did that early hands-on experience with application design and database administration prepare you for future IT leadership positions at Viacom and, ultimately, the CIO role with the City of Burbank?

A: Well, I started on a service desk at the entry levels in IT. And I've been lucky enough to have grown up through all aspects of it. I think climbing that ladder one rung at a time let me experience all the disciplines of technology. It enabled me to see the forest through the trees, the big picture. It taught me how to design operations, develop a strategy, and equipped me with a vision to incorporate it all. And now I can thoughtfully pull together a clear plan for how to run an organization, understand how to innovate, how to drive change through both a specific business unit and an organization. Experience is what best prepared me to lead.

Q: One of your focal points has always been the importance of aligning IT governance with an organization's business strategy. What are some of the practical ways IT teams accomplish this goal, and how vital is the relationship-building component that accompanies that synchronicity?

A: I think the most practical way to accomplish this is to focus on the people. Focus on the people developing the strategy and look at how their business is trying to implement it. Because the most vital thing is to be in alignment with the shared goal, in alignment with the people you're partnering with. You have to be a true partner with the business. The technology is the secondary piece. The technology is what you use to try to find the solution to the problem the business is trying to solve. And those business problems don't always stay the same. They change. They change based on economic conditions. They change based on market conditions. They may change based on who might be occupying the seat that you're trying to partner with.

So, you have to stay close, and you have to stay connected. That allows you to stay aligned. Then you can figure out the solutions that are going to help solve that particular business problem. You have to be agile. You have to be able to switch directions. When the business changes direction, you have to be able to switch direction. And I think too often, IT organizations, they don't stay connected. They believe that they're trying to solve this business strategy. That they're trying to solve the business' problems.

But then the business problems change, the strategies change, and they're suddenly not connected. Eventually, they're heading down the wrong direction for another three to six months, which is a lifetime in technology.

Not only do I try to stay aligned with my business partners, but I also require my teams to keep aligned. My direct reports, for example, I've aligned with the executives of the city. My direct reports each have between four and six departments that they need to be aligned with. And they're required to meet with the executives of their department regularly to make sure that they're staying aligned, and they're moving in the right direction. I also talk periodically with these city executives to make sure we're aligned.

Where does that help the most? Well, it's less likely, for example, that the Parks and Recreation department will try to implement a smart irrigation system without the help and expertise of the technology team. And sometimes, they're not purposely trying to avoid this collaboration, but they don't recognize the opportunity. They don't think of the value that we can bring to this business problem that they're trying to solve. They're not thinking of the technology that we can introduce, or they may be thinking of technology, but they don't necessarily think of us as the ones who can best bring that solution to fruition.

Q: *You've traveled frequently around the globe for business and pleasure. How have those experiences influenced your strategies and approaches to managing people or the design of systems and programs? To borrow a phrase, should you act locally but think globally when it comes to an IT vision?*

A: The greatest things I've learned come directly from my experiences interfacing with different cultures and seeing the special ways that people approach problems. How people work with one another. How people ultimately analyze those problems. I think it's very consequential because every problem is not a nail, so every solution can't be a hammer. If you don't have a good appreciation for different ways of seeing things, different approaches towards problems, then you're not able to choose the right tools from your toolkit. It prevents you from being able to see new ways of solving problems.

Just being open to experiencing those different cultural challenges opens you up to seeing those opportunities. It helps support and promote innovation and new ways of defining solutions. In terms of thinking globally and acting locally, when I was at Viacom, we coined a term, maybe we didn't conceive it, or somebody borrowed it from somewhere, but the term was "glocal." Glocal because people see and experience their own world, and their world is always local. In a lot of cases, laws and regulations are very local. But, to scale, you have to think on a larger spectrum. To serve a global company, you have to think globally. So, what you do is that you first define governance. You define overarching policies for how you're going to attack problems and then, within that framework that you've defined, you determine local policies to attack the local problem that you have to deal with. Approach it from a top-down perspective.

Q: Now that you're in the public sector, your customers aren't just consumers, they're citizens and public servants. What's the difference between developing IT solutions for private entities versus public ones? Are there any common themes?

A: The main difference I've gleaned is that in a public organization, we're not developing products that we're selling to people. We're not trying to grow markets. Our market is our community. We're not creating or manufacturing anything. What we're delivering are our services across the board. We are a service organization. Our product is the service we provide. Our effort has to be on improving, scaling, making those services efficient. That's the biggest focus as opposed to how to develop a product best. We do market ourselves in a sense, but it's not a physical product. We don't have, necessarily, supply chains for an item. We have supply chains for the services that we provide. That's the biggest difference.

In developing our IT frameworks, it doesn't necessarily translate to a different approach. It's just a difference in what we're focusing on. We're providing a service as opposed to say distributing a film. So, developing those frameworks is very similar, and the concepts apply to address the challenges of a small city.

I talked earlier about thinking glocally for a large multinational corporation, but I don't have to think glocally in this role. I do, however, have to serve 15 entirely different businesses. It's really 15 altogether different business units within a small city. I have a utility whose service is providing electricity and water for the citizens in the city. That's completely different than a police force that's focused on law enforcement, which is entirely different than a public works organization focused on building and maintaining streets and streetlights. Two entirely different businesses, if you will. So, when I'm developing a framework for a city, it has to be an overarching framework that can serve these diverse business units. Yet when we focus on a specific business unit, we have to zone in on the solutions within that framework that best help that particular service that the business unit is providing.

Q: Your education continued well beyond your initial degree work, leading to a SCRUM master and PMP certification. In today's competitive career landscape, how have these credentials aided your professional development, and what designations do you advise others seeking IT leadership roles pursue?

A: My perspective is a little different here than some of my peers. Yes, continued education is an absolute necessity. You have to continue to learn. You have to continue to grow. As people get older, they naturally get accustomed to their ways, but sometimes they get too comfortable. They don't look to learn and grow. Hence, you get guys and gals that have been a mainframe administrator for their entire career, and they stay a mainframe administrator until they retire.

My willingness to learn is what provided me with my first big opportunity in technology because, at my first company, we were a mainframe shop for government contract pricing applications. When mainframes became too expensive to maintain, our business decided to move into open systems like Unix. I worked with a team of mainframe engineers, and I was a service desk guy. When we started that transition to Unix, not all of the mainframe people wanted to get onboard. That opened the door for me. I started learning Unix and became a system administrator. I went to Unix systems administration training courses. I bought books, and I began to read. Within a couple of years, I became the lead on the project. When we transitioned that application from the mainframe, I became the go-to person. It set me up.

I learned then, early in my career, that the worst thing that we can do was get stuck in our ways. Get stuck in the technology that we focus in. Get stuck in the way with which we conduct our careers. So, I've always embraced that principle. What I don't necessarily embrace on its face are certifications because I've known a lot of certified idiots.

Some folks have ten certifications, but practically they can't accomplish much of anything because they live inside of a book. You need that book to learn the concepts and methodologies. But to transition that to real life, you need to deploy it in real life, to find out what works and what doesn't. What works out of the book. What doesn't work? What applies? What doesn't apply? Once you do that, you need to get back into the books and keep learning. You've got to figure out what's my next step. What's the next step in the journey to continuous improvement? What's the next step in the journey of both personal, professional growth?

When books aren't enough for me, if something isn't sitting well, or sticking with me, then sometimes I'll take a class. That class may or may not result in a certification. But I tell you what, in the end, I can sit down and have that conversation about Lean Six Sigma principles with the green belt or the black belt, whether I have the green belt or the black belt certification or not, right? That's my goal in my career. Now, certifications do certainly help when you're moving from one job to the next. If you don't have the credentials, it may dent your resume. But if you can get in the door and sit down and talk about that subject as well as anybody else that might have the certification, then the knowledge is as much, if not more valuable than the paper.

Q: Is there any opportunity to monetize public data, or do public entities avoid doing that? Amazon, as part of its headquarters search, was accused of using that project to harvest city data about urban housing and planning.

A: Perhaps, but I don't think so and let me tell you why. In general, everything we do, every email we write, every plan we develop, every policy we write, can all be acquired with a public records request. Everything we do has to be available. There's very little that is done either in a local, state or federal government that isn't accessible publicly or that can't be obtained with a request. Amazon or anybody else can get that type of information in one way or another. There are very few restrictions on what data a city is not obligated to share with whoever asks. There are some rules and policies around getting that data, but the truth is anybody can ask for anything from the city, and we're usually obligated to provide it. There are very few legal ramifications that prevent us from sharing that kind of information.

For a city to consider monetizing that information, it's

counter to what we do. We collect revenue, but the revenue that we collect is intended for the provisioning of the services that we provide, right? We're not profit-motivated by any means. There's a double-edged sword to that, because not being profit-motivated sometimes results in a city not being as efficiency-motivated, not necessarily trying to find ways to do more with less or save costs. But not being profit-motivated also means you can't go chase dollars. If you're chasing dollars, it should be for funding the service that you're providing.

Q: What about using artificial intelligence? Is that technology being adequately leveraged in civic pursuits?

A: I'd say we're still in the beginning stages, in the infancy of all that. I have a few strategic initiatives that I'm driving for the City of Burbank. And I'm trying to stay ahead of where most of the cities are and trying to catch up where we might be behind. When I catch up, I want to go beyond. Of course, I'm happily sharing everything that I learn, everything I'm doing with all of our sister cities. I've taken several steps, written several policies and proposals and presentations. I did a smart city presentation for the city that got us to start thinking about where we stand on that journey and how we can continue to become a smarter city.

I'm trying to push the envelope. And one of those areas includes data analytics. We're building a data and analytics practice here in the City of Burbank where it didn't exist before so that we can find ways to better utilize the data we have. Because you're right, in that cities have a ton of data, but we haven't always put a lot of thought into how we can better use it to improve the services that we provide. That could be anything from improving the traffic flow to increasing the revenue from parking. Or even predictive criminal enforcement, if you will. For example, if there are ways you can determine where a crime may occur, then you can better deploy your resources.

Q: Do you think that runs up against some privacy issues?

A: We'll see. I think there's going to be a journey. There's going to be a pendulum swing. I'd say the pendulum is swinging towards less privacy, at least in public spaces, but there's going to be some problems with that, and it will begin to swing back.

Q: Do you think it perhaps could lead to less privacy in public spaces yet more in private ones?

A: That is precisely what I expect to see, and I'll give you an example. The camera systems that we have in the City of Burbank are pretty strategically placed, but not very widespread. In another prominent Southern California city, they have pervasive camera systems. They started to focus on major thoroughfares and not necessarily within their residential areas. But what they found is that when they catch crimes and can use the video evidence in their prosecution successfully, in those neighborhoods, people initially didn't want cameras there. But when they started to experience burglaries, people would come back and ask if there was any video evidence, and they didn't. Naturally, those residents began to request video systems. Now, that city is at a point that if a burglary happens, and they don't catch it on video, they're almost obligated to deploy new cameras. That's a prime example of how technology can quickly change people's perspectives.

Chapter 6

Driving Conversations Around Telematics

John Danenberger, Corporate Counsel, State Farm Insurance
Topics: Telematics, Autonomous Vehicles

"Telematics is going to solve a lot of problems because you're realizing that things aren't the same way they were 50 years ago."
John Danenberger

John Danenberger, CPCU, is Corporate Counsel at State Farm Insurance and specializes in addressing issues around telematics. He served in the US Army and is licensed to practice law in Texas and Illinois. He received his bachelor's from DePaul University, a master's from UCL, and his JD from Loyola University Chicago School of Law.

Q: John, our cars are smartphones on wheels, tracking vehicle location, performance, and driver behavior. Data points include unique identifiers, breaking, and acceleration habits. How exactly are auto insurers leveraging telematics?

A: Right now, app-driven insurers are better at capitalizing on this new technology than traditional insurance companies. Insurers like Lemonade, Root, State Farm's Highroad and Blue Owl are using telematics to price each individual's risk exposure in real-time. That's huge for the customer because they're able to affect their premium by just driving safely. They can say, look, "I'm a better citizen by driving safer, and I get a premium discount."

Q: Who owns data collected by vehicular telematics technology, and who can access it?

A: The growing trend is to say that the driver owns the data. But what is the driver signing away when they buy a new car that's equipped with telematics? Honda, for example, could easily put a clause in their sales contract that says, by signing this deal and doing your financing through us, you agree to give up data ownership. I would say a majority of customers are willing to sign over some of that privacy as long as their own life is taken care of swifter, easier in the event of a claim, or an emergency where they need a tow or just a can of gas. Once data leaves the car and exists in a satellite cloud space, then it probably is owned by the original equipment manufacturer. I strongly support the larger insurance companies partnering with manufacturers so that we can share that data. We can help service our customers faster and accurately if we get that data immediately.

Q: Do you expect to see regulatory interest around telematics and data privacy changing?

A: I think in the next five years we'll start seeing companies enter markets underpriced or undervalued and then have to raise rates significantly within a 12 to 18 month period. We've already seen it in Rhode Island and California, and we'll see it in other states as these kinds of emergent, app-driven insurance companies enter more markets. That's when the regulators are going to come in and say things like, "Well, wait a minute. We saw your initial application. We approved your initial application before this rate change. Let's see the math that's making you justify such a rate increase." States want to be innovative and business-friendly. On the other side, they're going to have to explain their decision-making.

Q: What obstacles are blocking innovation and the adoption of autonomous vehicle technology?

A: The short answer is federal agencies cannot agree on a model bill, and they are slow to speak on autonomous vehicle technology. The agencies themselves are not aligned, and there's not a unified message from the federal government.

Q: Can telematics help solve issues of equity and environmental concerns?

A: They absolutely can. We've already seen what insurance companies have done with telematics, and we've already seen people using their cars less, which is good for the environment. We're seeing our drivers become more responsible. Telematics is going to solve a lot of problems because you're realizing that things aren't the same way they were 50 years ago. Just because some people didn't settle down, buy a house, and have a family, doesn't necessarily mean they have more risk exposure than someone that might have done those things.

Q: What opportunities do you see for the professionals seeking emergent technology-related positions within large enterprises?

A: The room for growth is massive. The next 10 to 20 years are going to be exciting for professionals that want to do pricing, contracting, and legal work in this space. Professionals that can price these interesting products and identify risks companies need to cover for both customers and employees will be able to draft contracts in a clever, yet straightforward way. The sky's the limit.

Q: How did you make the transition from a military career to working in corporate America?

A: I came out of law school in Chicago, began working at an intellectual property firm, and had the good fortune to speak in many courtrooms in Illinois and Virginia. When I got to the JAG Corps, they made me a trial attorney. I would have preferred to have done defense work, but they made me a prosecutor. While

I continued to get good results or at least satisfying results in the courtroom, the work did kind of way on my mind a bit. And when my time as a prosecutor was coming to an end, they asked me what I wanted to do. I said, "Convoys." So, they made me the head of claims for Eurocom over in Germany.

For the armed services, there are only four statutes that govern our claims process. So, after you know or are familiar with those, they send you on your way, and you're able to counsel operations that are using convoys and transportation along the border. Back in 2013-14, there was a buildup along what used to be known as the Eastern Wall. We were convoying massive operations through Germany and into Poland, and a lot of that was done with emergent technologies that were not available in the private sector. The lead convoy truck would have a human driver, and the six, seven, eight trucks that followed that lead truck wouldn't necessarily need a human behind the wheel. We were able to move very efficiently, very effectively through two or three countries at a time!

Once I'd been satisfied with my service to my country, I wanted to continue being involved in this area in any way I could. I was looking for an insurance company that was willing or already involved with having an app that was driven towards safety. State Farm was one.

I'd like to see more programs start incorporating telematics data. For instance, the State Farm grid could know whether an erratic driver was two miles down the road and be able to warn customers and say, "Hey, it's close to midnight. We see a driver two miles down the road that's made eight lane changes in 40 seconds. You may want to pull over."

Chapter 7

Tapping into Africa's Potential

**Amb-Dr. Oyedokun Ayodeji Oyewole, Chairman,
Institute of Information Management**
Topics: Information Management, Upward Mobility

*"Having a society where quality records and information can be
easily accessed must be a priority..."*
Amb-Dr. Oyedokun Ayodeji Oyewole

Amb-Dr. Oyedokun Ayodeji Oyewole, FIIM, ERMS, RMEM,
FIRMS is the Chairman of the Board at the Institute of Information
Management based in Nigeria. Before leading the institute, he
served in senior IT roles for Swedish firms and consulted on
cybersecurity needs for the oil and gas industry. He received his
BSc in Computer Science from Lagos State University.

*Q: Amb-Dr. Oyedokun, your work developing new practitioners in
Records and Computer Science fields in Africa is substantial and
encouraging. You have empowered your students to harness their
analytical skills, engage in professional development, and seize
opportunity. What inspired you to start building a community of
skilled practitioners that could make a difference in their communities?*

A: My journey started in 2004 with a tremendous vision and
mission. This was at a time when only a few organizations in Africa
were implementing data science and information management
technology. With the vast opportunities in those areas coupled
with the societal challenges faced by the continent, I saw the
need for us to bolster the demand for proper management and
security of records in both public and private organizations. A
huge chunk of organizations was still struggling with managing

59

physical records and certainly not prepared for electronic documents. Poverty, corruption, and a lack of employment opportunities were crippling.

In analyzing all of this, I felt the only meaningful solution to both alleviating suffering and empowering people was through the advancement of this industry, information management, neglected for decades in Africa. Having a society where quality records and information can be easily accessed must be a priority in the face of several challenges ranging from lack of government support, inadequate legislation, poorly trained professionals and practitioners, to the absence of standards and necessary tools for adequate data governance.

Q: Most people around the world don't realize that many parts of Africa, especially in Nigeria, finally have sophisticated infrastructures despite being considered developing nations. The history of Africa is varied and rich, with much of its potential still yet to be unlocked. What if anything do you feel is unique to African nations that you might not find in places like the United Kingdom or the United States?

A: Opportunities in Nigeria are still blossoming, and there is a lot of potential and talent yet to be tapped. I think what we see in Nigeria, especially, but other parts of Africa as well, reflects a belief by young people that it's becoming very possible to pursue success in a professional capacity. They carry a deep resolve to take their careers to the next level and make their lives better, despite a myriad of social and economic challenges less prevalent in the West. That's what inspires me the most.

Q: You spent quite some time working for Chevron Nigeria Limited on its Agura Independent Power Project designing IT systems. Nigeria's oil reserves are substantial, and as this sector develops, just like in the United States, there are social and environmental issues impacted by this progress. How much are projects such as those affected by laws and regulations in African nations, and what trends do you expect in the African regulatory landscape over the next five or ten years?

A: The regulatory environment in Nigeria is complex, creating challenges even for companies that strive hard to be compliant! There's legislation to regulate almost every area of economic activity. The pro-transparency, anti-corruption inclination of present administrations are seen as helping ensure accountability and good governance. That means empowered regulators are comfortable with coming down hard on breaches of local regulation. However, there hasn't been as much impact compared to other financial, telecommunications, and energy sectors operating in other parts of the world.

Yet amidst the mix of regulatory change and remaining instability, we do see opportunities for organizations to advance their local positioning and risk management approach. Performing necessary compliance audits and investing and internal capacity-building around compliance issues is being achieved. In Africa, I believe companies should learn to prioritize engagement and seek to build long-lasting interaction not only with regulators but across a broader base of public sector stakeholders. Engagement will intensify the understanding of regulators' priorities and facilitate dialogue that will ultimately improve policy formulation, and consequently help organizations to shape the ethical business environment around their operations.

Q: You have hosted a plethora of international business leaders at your conferences to bring new ideas to Africa. What kinds of contributions are Information Age professionals in the rest of the world making to support the development of these professions in Africa?

A: A lot is happening in terms of development in the global information management space, which I think Africa is yet to integrate into, realize, or benefit from fully. Nevertheless, some professionals and organizations like the Information and Records Management Society (IRMS), the International Records

Management Trust (IRMT), and the Information Governance Initiative (IGI) have been of tremendous inspiration and support to the development of our industry and job seekers in Africa. There are lots of opportunities for international professionals who might be interested in exploring, including business and consultancy services here. The records and information management profession of the 21st century is one for the brave-hearted, exciting, and with further potential than ever before.

Part II Less is More

"It is not important to make many pictures, but that I have one picture right."
Piet Mondrian

As brands and consumers develop a deeper awareness of the importance of protecting their data, the idea of sharing *less* is becoming a *more* prudent, preferential, and effective approach to governance. In fact, in domains like privacy, content management, and application development, data minimization has become a dominant design strategy. An emphasis on discretion and privacy is nothing new, but it has gained relevancy following the dawn of social media, a cultural and technological revolution that encourages individuals and businesses alike to share everything about themselves.

The affordability of digital storage and ease of data transferability has enabled technology to transform social interactions fundamentally, but the consequences of ineffective data stewardship are quickly catching up with the conveniences at our fingertips. Identity theft, ransomware, and other malicious hacking events are taking a toll on our businesses and our personal lives. The proposed remedy for these problems has come in the form of new laws and regulations, such as the General Data Protection Requirement (GDPR) and its derivatives throughout Asia and the Americas. We see the pendulum starting to swing back toward privacy as a result of related penalties, reputational damage, and growing security threats. In software development, data minimization has become a preeminent design methodology.

Yet despite new rules directing how businesses should document, disclose, audit, and defend the use of our information, in the end, it is the individual's responsibility to filter out the deluge of data. To guard against data that attempts to inundate, persuade, and obligate our time regularly. Its frequency and intensity are unparallel in human history and eat away at our natural inclination to pause, contemplate, and deduce. There's nowhere to run or hide from the status quo.

This new paradigm we find ourselves in necessarily requires us to selectively amplify when our voices need to be heard and be mindfully methodical about identifying and seizing opportunities amidst the inbound cacophony. To truly capitalize on the first lesson given in this book, *Gaps are Opportunities*, we must regularly exercise our will to avoid impulsive and lesser offers while navigating toward greater lasting rewards. And we must remain disciplined in this cadence at work and in the home. Clarity, brevity, and directness will increasingly be the in-demand soft skills that advance our agenda and our careers.

Finding the bottom line

Less is More isn't just about privacy, though, or how we conduct ourselves, it's a better way of doing business now that a majority of brands are dependent on the currency of information. From a corporate governance and project management perspective, reactive management techniques, resource expansion, or throwing money at a problem isn't a safe or cost-effective bet anymore. Have they ever been? Indeed, anybody who has worked in a regulated industry has witnessed how easily large organizations repeatedly squander budgets to check a box symbolically. Most sourcing professionals, when they're honest, can tell you horror stories about statements of work that ended up resulting in nothing more than an imaginary bill of goods and even vulnerabilities. That's because (especially in the era of big data) without clear and concise goals, roadmaps, and communication strategies, the more bureaucratic a solution gets, the less likely the results will be favorable. That common disorder also affects an entity, whether it is public or private, regardless of the complexity of the underlying problem.

How exactly does a *Less is More* strategy make the best teams in the business world run so smoothly? The idea itself almost seems counterintuitive in today's business climate, but that's because we've grown so accustomed to information overload that we instinctively over-respond, reactively, to the slightest outside pressure and regulation. Companies that exercise restraint can still respond effectively to immediate concerns and market shifts, but they do so by simplifying corporate policies, prioritizing business goals, and communicating with the same maturity. That doesn't mean there isn't a place for precision and quality assurance, but far too often we see micromanagement murdering the mothers of invention.

While working as executives at Fortune 500 companies, we observed closely the tangible benefits of careful, restrained strategic planning, a light senior managerial footprint, and the results of executing capstone projects using moderated cadence. We've also witnessed the effects of doing exactly the opposite and the stresses it places on even the most patient, resilient knowledge workers, and team leaders. Over time, as a result of some tough lessons also experienced by some colleagues in this book, we began to witness and value the results of a *Less is More* strategy. Finding the right balance of restraint and proactivity is an essential skill for all agents of change in the Information Age. This is especially true in the era of data protection and inevitable data breaches.

If we take this concept a step further and think about it in the context of the Net Promotor Score, or NPS, in gauging customer experience, we glean a prime example of the need for simplification and balance. Most organizations end up doing the same thing with this generally useful tool. They survey the hell out of everything, build enormous data lakes, and end up not even being able to see the forest through the trees. The obsessiveness drives customers and employees crazy besides the fact that it creates an analytics nightmare if not correctly implemented. Ultimately, most companies settle on that one question, *how likely are you to recommend, buy, stay, etc.*? That's what we're all trying to do in finding an opportunity amidst the gaps in our various programs and products. We're trying to drill down to the bottom line, the main objective, the motivating factor, the differentiator. Drilling a thousand holes in the wall usually just gets you an expensive new drywall project. Some answers and suspicions about the customer experience can still best be understood and confirmed by just listening to your actual customers, either face to face or directly over the phone or by email.

To help find and maintain the right balance and avoid this deluge of garbage data, our best teams and leaders insist that guiding principles, policies, and directives governing data are clear and concise. That may seem obvious, but it isn't always evident in practice, especially in an era of oversharing or within a work culture that worships the Almighty CYA (cover your ass). Straightforwardness is not an easy sell today to a population with a 144-character attention span and one that's less inclined to comply with communication in traditional ways. To complicate matters, we commonly see legal departments and advisors addressing the governance aspects of policy, who know a lot about the law, yet very little about how to write an operational rule. This is a familiar theme and common challenge we all face both in our personal and professional lives.

To be strategically selective with our words, our actions and our expectations runs contrary to the human nature of a large segment of the workforce and consumers. It's also what makes you stand out.

Back on the road

In the first section, *Gaps are Opportunities,* we introduced you to an entrepreneur who made a killing seizing on opportunity along the interstate following World War I. The roads we travel today are filled with businesses like his, symbolizing much more than just the trade they serve. Perhaps the most famous business that exemplifies the value of the *Less is More* strategy is In-N-Out Burger, a restaurant chain with over 300 locations founded in 1948. The secret of their success is attributed to the simplicity of their menu, which has not changed much in the seven decades since its inception. What observers fail to realize is that while *Less is More* has made that storied food hub tremendously successful and scalable, it's anything but extraordinary or original. In fact, it's a fundamental strategy that powers small businesses everywhere.

Thousands of miles from the nearest In-N-Out, but just a short drive from Mechanicsburg, Ohio, there's a family diner just as loved by the locals there as In-N-Out is to Los Angelenos. Crabill's Hamburgers Shoppe serves up two items: sliders and home-made potato chips, cash only. People drive from miles around to sit at the six-seat counter restaurant, waiting in lines outside without complaint for the legendary lunch. Yet despite numerous opportunities to franchise the business, the family-run company has been resisting expansion since 1927. They're comfortable with their profitable lot, and there's nothing wrong with that.

The secret of Crabill's success is no different from that of In-N-Out. *Less is More* is a proven strategy that enables businesses to effectively execute on their mission and focus on keeping operations running smoothly.

Creating digital boundaries

The *Less is More* strategy and mindset are also useful for separating work demands from the burdens and blessings of life's responsibilities. After all, our first priorities in life remain our physical health and mental well-being. Those prerequisites for happiness can hardly be satisfied with the success of our careers. We once referred to this careful dance as "work-life balance," but recently, emboldened by the ubiquitous nature of personal devices, a new euphemism has arisen. It's designed to normalize our workaholic tendencies and is labeled "work-life integration."

Once an obscure term, the concept has gained traction because, at this point in history, we're all enduring an unnatural overlap between our personal and professional lives. Despite broad adoption, businesses are already learning that cultures blurring the line between work and home life often results in an encroachment that makes workforces less productive. It's a trend obfuscated by the marketing and metrics waved in our faces by the fit-bit-digerati.

The reality of work-life integration is made possible, and accessible to all, by the technological wonders that promote and accompany the Information Age. These offerings are marketed as must-have tools of convenience, advertised as essential life-hacks that, in many regards, even make us better people! In some instances, you literally cannot live without them.

Yet contrary evidence is abundant, both statistical and devilishly anecdotal (in the case of the death-by-selfie) that proves how this total immersion in all things digital is hollowing us out emotionally and intellectually. We are no longer slaves to Pharaoh and relegated to pushing stones, but today we feel like we're inching forward, restrained by invisible digital leashes, breaking up the leaps, bounds, and depths of our attention spans. Modern technological lifestyles even seem to polish away the rough and creative contours of our character. We are frequently robbed of our internal monologues and instead given social media profiles and hashtags, mere shadows of what we represent and mean to others.

We needn't run to an isolated cabin in the woods and pen a manifesto blaming innovation for all of our woes. We do need to draw clear battle lines with our favorite robots, lest we end up a mirror of them. It bears repeating. Less technology in our personal life equals more, long, meaningful breaths before we meet our maker.

Work-life integration is dramatized in Cecil DeMille's classic *The Ten Commandments*. Remember the famous scene where a worker is about to be trampled by a giant stone moved by "her colleagues." Moses' character, played by Charlton Heston, strides down from his managerial pedestal to save the poor soul, who later turns out is his mother! It's a metaphor for how easily, regularly, and unfairly we put work before family, friends, and our well-being. And when work negatively impacts others, it is demonstrably immoral.

I first learned about this 24/7 mindset by a CIO, who boasted, "Say I'm on a flight to Hawaii with my family for the weekend, and I've got to approve a purchase order for half-a-million. I can do it right here from my iPhone!" Well, that's fitting, but it highlights the disconnect between those who have the world at their disposal and those who get interrupted with an email from their boss every weekend. The same technology fix that feeds the workaholic is now invading everyone's space. It's affecting their partner, their children, their social circle, people on the road. Do we want to subject ourselves to this type of digital bondage?

Whether humanity is building Pyramids or iPads, imposed upon us or of our own making, an obsessive and aggressive approach to time-management will ultimately usurp what little personal, spontaneous, and family time we still have left. Does anybody living today hope for a gravestone that reads, "I wish I had worked, texted, emailed my customer more?"

Ironically, this new digital bondage is reminiscent of the days when men and women of all ages built the Pyramids until they dropped dead. Sure, those grandiose sand tombs still stand as a testament to architecture and ingenuity, but they will also always represent a chapter in history when there was seldom a break from work. Luckily today, we have a choice.

We must stand firmly behind the importance of rest and personal space. Sure, working remotely through technology has given us flexibility. There's no denying that. But ideas like work-life integration have adversely impacted the very relationships and working-conditions they were meant to improve.

In the Jewish faith, observers believe that the Sabbath, a day of rest, is a cornerstone of not just spiritual growth, but what ultimately may lead to success in other areas of one's life. Most cultures share this value, but as it erodes across the globe in the modern era, and the lines between work and rest are worn away, we all suffer together. Create digital boundaries to separate work and life to free yourself from that digital bondage.

Walk before you run

Lastly, *Less is More* is also a business approach analogous to servant leadership, one that mentors by exemplifying measured discipline and a rational expectation setting for business partners, teams, and customers. It's based on the understanding that we don't want to overwhelm our already overwhelmed audience and peers. Our chosen cadence, especially in large, complex organizations, requires a nuanced understanding of company culture, its maturity level, and its appetite for change. Those considerations shape our strategies as we plan and adjust our change management plans and the technology strategies we select, or these days, select us. Ultimately our cadence will influence the footprint we hope to leave. How do we expect our message to get across if we don't serve as its example? Do we want to race to the finish line like the hare or be deliberate in our strategic and cultural choices as we move forward like the tortoise?

Company culture isn't something we individually determine, but it's a basic pillar we must build upon and may need to influence to nurture opportunities and get shared goals accomplished. A company that's behind the curve on innovation, or has slipped a little off the tracks shouldn't be treated as suffering from a deeply rooted cultural problem but rather perceived as one ripe for change. How we respond to inefficiencies, gaps, audit findings, and weaknesses in product offerings or team performance can make all the difference between an organization hostile to change or one welcoming to it.

In the modern era, we see companies rushing into paradigm-shifting projects like digital transformation and quickly being served up a big plate of *not buying it*. Groups that pick up the mantle of digital transformation, excited by its potential, end up running around in circles, hurriedly setting up committees, imposing rules, writing up new guidelines, buying shelf-ware, and sprinting towards what they think will be early wins. Yet change management and digital transformation is not merely a race.

A successful transformation necessitates a thoughtful assessment of the existing cultural, regulatory, operational landscape. Change agents today need to immerse themselves in understanding a firm's technical capability and thresholds. Only then can its leaders develop a wise, aspirational, and reasonable plan. A planned yet flexible cadence covers essential bases and addresses the cultural needs of the business. It does not dump barrels of whiskey on its known drunks.

A clear, salient, and targeted executive-level strategy around change and innovation:

- **Presents:** opportunities for better governance to avoid fines and litigation exposure
- **Helps:** to reduce expenses and monetize the information or product lifecycle
- **Fosters:** trust to enhance employee, business partner, and customer experiences

Instead of rushing in with a million ideas and every cook on hand, smart organizations and its leaders are better served with this empirically proven *Less is More* approach. Find the opportunity in between the gaps, facilitate honest discussions to achieve your goals, and don't lose sight of results. *No kitchen sink required.*

Taking the next steps

In the following set of interviews, we'll put on our cap and gown and get schooled on the origins and implications of privacy from a professor who wrote the first modern casebook on the subject. After that, things get a little litigious as we take a deep dive into eDiscovery with the co-creator of the Electronic Discovery Resource Model. We'll spend some time in Germany with one of the fathers of enterprise content management and examine how the nature of work will be forever changed by the technology we're just getting to know. That insight should prepare us for our next adventure into digital transformation with a Microsoft MVP. Next, we'll take a look into how the world's largest information management company is applying AI and analytics to sort out our old records. We'll end up at the bottom line, by keeping it simple with advice from a renowned expert in the global information governance industry.

Chapter 8

Professing Principles of Digital Ethics and Privacy

Dr. Anita L. Allen, Vice Provost and Professor, University of Pennsylvania

Topics: Privacy, Social Media

"For me, trust has to be earned. It's not something that can be demanded or pulled out of a drawer and handed over. And the more government or the business sector shows genuine regard and respect for peoples' privacy in their actions, as well as in their word and policies, the more that trust will come into being."

Dr. Anita L. Allen

Dr. Anita Allen serves as Vice Provost for Faculty and Henry R. Silverman Professor of Law and Philosophy at the University of Pennsylvania. Dr. Allen is a renowned expert in the areas of privacy, data protection, ethics, bioethics, and higher education, having authored the first casebook on privacy law and has been awarded numerous accolades and fellowships for her work. She earned her JD from Harvard and both her Ph.D. and master's in philosophy from the University of Michigan.

Q: Dr. Allen, a few years ago you spoke to the Aspen Institute and offered a prediction that "our grandchildren will resurrect privacy from a shallow grave just in time to secure the freedom, fairness, democracy, and dignity we all value... a longing for solitude and independence of mind and confidentiality..." Do you still feel that way, and if so, what will be the motivating factors for reclaiming those sacred principles?

A: Yes, I believe that very hopeful prediction will come true because there's an increasing sense in the general public of the extent to which we have perhaps unwittingly ceded our privacy controls to the corporate sector, and in addition to that, to the government. I think the Facebook problems that have been so much in the news around Cambridge Analytica have made us sensitive and aware of the fact that we are, by simply doing things we enjoy, like communicating with friends on social media, putting our lives in the hands of strangers.

And so, these kinds of disclosures, whether they're going to be on Facebook or some other social media business, are going to drive the next generation to be more cautious. They'll be circumspect about how they manage their personal information, leading to, I hope, eventually, a redoubled effort to ensure our laws and policies are respectful of personal privacy.

Q: How do we connect young people with those "sacred" principles when they're growing up in environments that encourage oversharing and lack appreciation for the internal monologue?

A: I think what is happening is that even without the private monologue, public events are creating a big exclamation point. Even the very young are learning that their communications, which they think of as private, are actually revealing information about them. Not just revealing information about the exact content of what they're talking about, but also revealing information about their tastes, their values, and their preferences and so forth that can be discerned through artificial intelligence.

The normative movement that I once felt was so important around public education, and education in the family remains so. But the headlines in the newspapers about data breaches and voluntary disclosures of data for commercial and political purposes, that kind of information, is out there in the public. It's teaching the next generation of college students and young people about the basis for being concerned about their information.

Q: Perhaps the next generation heeds the wisdom of their elders and avoids the career pitfalls and reputational consequences of exposing too much on the internet?

A: I do think that's it as well. Your original question was about my prediction that the future would see a restoration of concern about privacy. I believe that, yes, as experience shows the younger generation just what the consequences are of living your life in the public view and there will be a turnaround to some extent. To get people to focus on what they have to lose. It's not just that you could lose job opportunities. You could lose school admissions. You could lose relationship opportunities and the ability to find the right partner because your reputation is so horrible on social media.

All of those consequences are causing people to be a little more reserved. It may lead to a big turnaround when people finally get enough control over their understanding of those consequences that they activate their political and governmental institutions to do better by them.

Q: While our right to privacy isn't explicitly stated in the U.S. Constitution, it's reasonably inferred from the language in the amendments. Yet today, "the right to be forgotten" is an uphill battle. Some bad actors brazenly disregard a "right to be left alone," as defined by Justice Brandeis in 1890. Is legislation insufficient to protect privacy in the Information Age, or is the fault on the part of law enforcement and the courts?

A: I've had the distinct pleasure to follow developments in privacy law pretty carefully for the last 20 years, now approaching 30, and am the author or co-author of numerous textbooks on the right to privacy in the law, and so I'm familiar with the legal landscape. I can say from that familiarity that the measures we have in place right now are not adequate. It's because the vast majority of our privacy laws were written literally before the internet, and in some cases in the late 1980s or early 1990s or early 2000s as the world was vastly evolving. So yes, we do need to go back and refresh our electronic communications and children's internet privacy laws. We need to rethink our health privacy laws constantly. And all of our privacy laws need to be updated to reflect existing practices and technologies.

The right to be forgotten, which is a right described today as a new right created by the power of Google, is an old right that goes back to the beginning of privacy law. Even in the early 20th century, people were concerned about whether or not dated, but true information about people could be republished. So, it's not a new question, but it has a new shape. It would be wonderful if our laws and our common law could be rewritten so that the contemporary versions of old problems, and completely new issues brought on by global technologies, could be rethought in light of current realities.

Q: The Fourth Amendment to the Constitution was intended to protect Americans from warrantless search and seizure. However, for much of our history, citizens have observed as surveillance has become politically charged and easily abused. How would our founders balance the need for privacy, national security, and the rule of law today?

A: The fourth amendment is an amazing provision that protects persons from a warrantless search and seizure. It was designed to protect peoples' correspondence, letters, papers, as well as business documents from disclosure without a warrant. The idea of the government collecting or disclosing sensitive personal information about us was the same then as it is now. The fact that it's much more efficient to collect information could be described as almost a legal technicality as opposed to a fundamental shift.

I think that while the founding generation couldn't imagine the fastest computers we all have on our wrists and our desktops today, they could understand entirely the idea that a person's thoughts and conduct would be placed under government scrutiny. They could see that people would be punished by virtue of government taking advantage of access to documents never intended for them to see. So, I think they could very much appreciate the problem and why it's so important that we do something to restore some sense of balance between the state and the individual.

Q: Then, those amendments perhaps anticipated some of today's challenges?

A: Sure. Not in the abstract, but think of it in the concrete. If we go back to the 18th and 19th centuries, you will find some theorists speculating that someday there will be new inventions that will raise these types of issues. Warren and Brandeis talked specifically about new inventions and business methods. So, it's never been far from the imagination of our legal minds that more opportunities would come through technology. They anticipated technologies that would do the kinds of things once only done with pen and paper, things that can now be done in cars and with computers. It's a structurally identical problem. And so, while I do think our laws could be easily updated, including our constitutional laws, the constitutional principles are beautiful in part because fundamentally they do continue to apply even though times have changed quite a bit.

Some of the constitutional languages we find in other countries around ideas like human dignity, which is now applied to privacy regulations, shows that, to some extent, very general constitutional language can be put to other purposes.

Q: What region of the globe is the most lacking in privacy protections?

A: I would not purport to answer that question or even the question of which region of the world is best. I think a lot of people would point to Europe and say, "Oh, the European Union is clearly ahead of the United States! Or Canada is ahead here or there." To some extent the quality of privacy that people enjoy in a particular country is a function of their laws but also their customs and their mores, you know?

Q: *In a speech to the 40ᵗʰ International Data Protection and Privacy Commissioners Conference, you posited that "Every person in every professional relationship, every financial transaction and every democratic institution thrives on trust. Openly embracing ethical standards and consistently living up to them remains the most reliable ways individuals and businesses can earn the respect upon which all else depends." How do you facilitate trust, ethics, and morality in societies that have lost confidence in the authority of their institutions and have even begun to question their legitimacy?*

A: For me, trust has to be earned. It's not something that can be demanded or pulled out of a drawer and handed over. Unfortunately, the more draconian and unreasonable state actors behave respecting people's privacy, the less people will be able to generate the kind of trust that's needed. And the more government or the business sector shows genuine regard and respect for peoples' privacy in their actions, as well as in their word and policies, the more that trust will come into being.

I think that people have to begin to act in ways that make trust possible. I have to act in ways that make trust possible by behaving respectfully towards my neighbors, my family members, and my colleagues at work, and they the same toward me. The businesses that we deal with have to act in ways that are suggestive of respect for their customers and their vendors. Up and down the chain. That's what I think. There's no magic formula, but I do think there's some room for conversation for education in schools, in religious organizations, in NGOs, and policy bodies. There is room for conversations that enable people to find discourses about privacy, confidentiality, data protection that can be used when people demonstrate that they want to begin to talk together about the importance of respect for these standards.

It's surprising to me how often I'm asked to define privacy or define data protection. When we're at the point where experts in the field have to be asked to give definitions of key concepts, we're, of course, at a point where it's going to be hard to have conversations that can develop trust around these ideas. That's because people are not always even talking about the same thing. Or they don't even know what to talk about under the rubric. We're in the very early days of being able to generate trust around data protection, artificial intelligence, and the like because it's just too new.

Q: The technology is new, but the principles are almost ancient, aren't they?

A: Exactly. If we have clear conceptions about what we're concerned about, whether its data protection or what we mean by artificial intelligence, then those ancient principles can be applied to new situations effectively.

Q: Okay, but if we consider the idea respect is also a top-down issue, in terms of the influence of state actors and business leaders, isn't there an impact of the ethical high ground being eroded over time? If those at the top of the pyramid are behaving in ways that diminish the value of trust, how is that even fixed or reversed?

A: To some degree, the problems that we're facing around data privacy are not the result of bad behavior, they're the result of over-generalization or overuse of a small set of concerns as drivers of public policy. For example, if your job is national security, you might focus so much on that as a value that you don't consider other values that might countermand national security, like respect for privacy or respect for individuals.

A lot of policymakers ignore or undervalue privacy because they treat their interests or enterprise, whether it's public health, national security, police safety, or efficient education, as having a certain set of goals, and they don't see that there are meaningful competing priorities. They're not bad actors. They're just actors who are not focusing on the broader array of values that are pertinent to what they're doing.

If you're a hospital, yes, you worry about the accuracy of medical records and the importance of biomedical research. Yet you can't forget respect for dignity that would prevent you from human subject research abuses or privacy abuses. So, it's about balancing priorities and values. I don't agree that this is a question of bad actors versus good ones.

There are some bad actors, of course. I do sometimes think in the corporate realm. Companies know that they are taking advantage of peoples' information. They know that they're violating reasonable expectations of privacy or expectations of privacy, which, if the consumer were aware of what was going on, might affect their purchasing decisions. Those are the bad actors for me. Actors who know there are privacy interests at stake that the public might not be aware of, and they need to be constrained. They must not be allowed to keep information away from consumers or to lie about the information given to the public. I think we can regulate against that to some extent, and we can use our criminal and civil liability system to address and perhaps deter some of that bad conduct.

Q: *In a world where people have a little less shame about conduct, doesn't that somehow impact the general population's view of the exploitation of our data?*

A: It seems to me we have entered a phase where there's less shame, but a lot of that's OK because I think we can all agree that maybe in the past, we were a bit too ashamed of our sexuality, of our opinions. Being able to express ourselves freely is a good thing. I guess I'm not sure yet on where we are going because I'm thinking about, even like 50 years ago, when it would have been seen as uncouth to go out in public without your hat and gloves. We have to be careful that we don't think that everything that happens that's revealing is necessarily wrong in some absolute sense.

It's different to be sure. But what's a matter of not wearing your hat and gloves, and what's a matter of demeaning yourself? I certainly have been a strong advocate for moralizing about privacy and trying to get people to be more reserved and less willing to disclose when it comes to demeaning oneself. And I constantly use the example of Anthony Weiner as someone who, in public life, went too far, and not only disclosed but demeaned himself in the process. We do want to take precautions against that. But if it's just a matter of, "we used to wear white gloves to Sunday school, and now we don't..." If that's what we're talking about, then it's not that important.

Q: You served as an elder for the Presbyterian Church in your local community. Does faith or any other religious value play a role or influence how you educate students or dissect ethical issues like privacy in your professional capacity?

A: I think the religious traditions in which you were brought up or that you embrace, even if it's not explicit, implicitly affects what you recommend and what you're comfortable with. To be sure, I have tried to mine my religious traditions to find insight and guidance around privacy issues. I even collect passages from the Bible that show how ancient concerns about bodily disclosure and information disclosure prove how ancient they are. You can find some wonderful things in the Old and the New Testament in which people are struggling with disclosure issues.

At the same time, if my religious tradition taught me that men were superior to women and that women should be seen and not heard, I would hate to see those kinds of norms reproduced in public law. We can't let our religious traditions directly dictate the kinds of laws that we think should govern a diverse and open society. But certainly, as an individual, how we think about problems and values are affected by our religious backgrounds, and mine as well.

Q: *You studied dance in college and then practiced law after graduating from Harvard, but ultimately decided to dedicate your career to higher education, writing, and consulting. What inspired you to pursue an academic career, and what would you say are the lasting rewards?*

A: I think a love of reading and ideas guided my career. Reading, writing, and ideas, and independence governed my choices. As an academic, I get to be far freer than many employees are. I get to write what I want to write, to think about what I want to think, and to teach and to engage people in ideas, in university, and outside the university. Those things governed my choices.

I loved being a practicing lawyer, but you have to think about and deal with whatever problems the clients bring to you. You don't always have that freedom of choice of topic to focus on. Then when it comes to things like dance or the arts, well, I love the arts, but I think I've always felt a little frustrated about the inability to make writing and debate sort of central to those activities. I think I am more of a person of the mind than a person of the body ultimately.

Chapter 9

Discovering Data that Matters

George Socha, Esq., Managing Director, Binder Dijker Otte
Topics: eDiscovery, Business Process Management

"People are constantly trying to figure out the most effective ways to get their jobs done. If they have technical barriers in front of them, sometimes they succumb to the enticement to circumvent those with unauthorized approaches."
George Socha

George Socha, Esq. is a renowned industry thought leader and the Managing Director of Binder Dijker Otte's Technology and Business Transformation Services practice. He has authored numerous articles on eDiscovery and speaks to global audiences on its rapid evolution and distinct challenges. George is also the co-founder of the widely utilized Electronic Discovery Reference Model (EDRM), a framework outlining standards for the recovery and discovery of digital data. He earned his bachelor's in political science from the University of Wisconsin-Madison and his JD from Cornell.

Q: George, along with Tom Gelbmann, you made a groundbreaking contribution to the discipline of eDiscovery with the Electronic Discovery Reference Model (EDRM) in 2005. That conceptual tool to understand the eDiscovery process became the foundation for an organization based at the Judicial Institute at Duke Law. What inspired you to develop this comprehensive approach to data collection in the litigation process?

A: The key motivator for us, as we were gathering information for a survey and interviewing subjects, was that we began hearing a common theme. We heard it, especially from providers of electronic discovery services and software, who said to us something akin to…"You guys don't really understand what e-discovery is. It's what WE do. All of those people out there claiming to do electronic discovery, that's not eDiscovery at all." We heard that same line from people whose focus was preserving data. We heard it from people who spent the bulk of their time and effort processing data. We heard it from people who hosted the data. We heard it from the folks who were reviewing it and so on. We thought - well, *there is no possible way all of them are right* because they're coming up with completely conflicting definitions! So, we asked ourselves, "Is there anything out there that already describe this?"

We looked around and didn't find any widely accepted definition of eDiscovery that laid out the major conceptual steps involved. We said to ourselves, since we can't find anything out there, let's see if we can put something together. I went through my address book. We reached out and got a group of I think maybe 35 organizations and people who showed up at the first EDRM meeting in May of 2005. We thought we were taking on a one-year project at the most. We were going to come up with a straightforward, pragmatic definition or set of definitions and some basic steps for people to think about as they limped through electronic discovery. At that time, we had no idea that over a decade later, anybody would be paying any attention to the work we were doing.

Q: And now that model is an entire institution and brand at Duke. How did it find a home there?

A: Tom was retiring, and from my perspective, I felt I had perhaps overextended my stay as a primary driver of EDRM. I also was looking at making a transition from a solo practice to joining another organization. So, with that backdrop, Tom and I decided it was time to look for a new home for EDRM. It took us a while, but ultimately someone we both knew fairly well put us in touch with the folks at Duke. Once we connected with them, things moved fairly quickly. In the summer of 2016, Tom and I handed over the project to their law school.

Q: What do you see as the EDRM's most intrinsic benefit to the legal community?

A: The creation, and now the maintenance, of the EDRM diagram. That diagram, for the first time, provided a conceptual framework that people could use to break down the fundamental data discovery processes. They could break them down into manageable pieces and understand how the parts could better connect. It is meant to be a conceptual framework. We've adjusted it over the years. I think we are now on the seventh version. You can go to a page on the EDRM website and take a look at the prior versions and see the evolution. Since the original, we've added privacy, security, and risk components.

Q: Law firms and corporate legal departments must leverage EDRM the most. But when did it go from an operational tool to something that courts started digesting and referencing?

A: It's not clear when that happened. I'm pretty sure the courts were not the first ones to notice and start paying attention to the EDRM diagram and framework. I think that the first ones to pay attention were the service and software providers, law firms, and corporate legal departments. Probably not long after that, it moved to individuals in various governmental institutions, and then somewhere along the way, the framework, even if not explicitly so, started to be brought to the attention of judges.

When I say not explicitly so, what I mean is that attorneys arguing before them or submitting materials might never have said, "Here is the EDRM framework. Go to EDRM.net and see more." But they were using the language. They were talking about identification, preservation, collection, each of the boxes, starting with identification and moving to the right on the diagram. Using a combination of those terms, in a way, made it clear that the EDRM framework was the basis for their understanding. It became the best mechanism to use to convey the concepts. I think they picked up on the terminology and the concepts behind the framework, well before any judge cited the EDRM framework.

Q: You co-authored a paper with Saaya Shah entitled "Data Validation, Crucial Steps Towards Controlling and Understanding Your Data." The goal of these strategies is to home in on "data that matters." What are some of your observations about how these strategies have been leveraged in high profile investigations involving email and servers?

A: One familiar example of that historically are limitations related to the volume of email. As a user, your PST file has limits on its size. There might be limits in the system in terms of how old an email message can be and can continue to live in your account. Because of those limits, email messages will flush out of the systems pretty regularly. Because of the limitations of technology, at least historically, there haven't been many easy ways to categorize and retain messages based on content. Those capabilities weren't usually there, and as a result, people who felt they had very good and legitimate reasons to keep those messages found workarounds. For example, sometimes, that meant saving copies of PST's outside of a corporate system. People are constantly trying to figure out the most effective ways to get their jobs done. If they have technical barriers in front of them, sometimes they succumb to the enticement to circumvent those with unauthorized approaches.

Q: A few years ago, I heard about companies saying they'd get rid of email entirely with new technologies like social media. How do you think that has worked out?

A: It's simple. On that front, what I have seen is that rarely have efforts to replace one technology, with another technology been all that successful. And using social media instead of email is a good example. Instead, what I've seen is that people don't get rid of old systems so much as add to new ones. There are some exceptions. I think we probably see very few faxes these days, although faxes are commonly used in some narrow areas. For the most part, they've disappeared. Email is still very extensively used.

What has happened is that email is not the only platform that folks use, and for some organizations, it's no longer even the platform that gets the most traffic. I attended a conference a year or two ago with a presenter who said, "We took a look at our internal traffic, and now we've gotten more Slack messages back and forth than we do email messages internally." They didn't say anything about the volume of their communications with the outside world, which I suspect their email system still dominates.

Q: *You have jested that you were forced into the field of eDiscovery against your will following the deposition of an IT director. But do your own experiences as an attorney continue to inform your guidance as a consultant?*

A: I think that my experience as an attorney was and continues to be critical. I was a practicing lawyer, a litigator for 16 years. I want to say I was a trial lawyer, but I did not try enough cases ever to feel comfortable attaching that label to my name. And the most extended trial I participated in was four months. I did handle matters throughout their entire lifecycle. I drafted complaints, answers, prepared discovery requests, and responses — over ten thousand of them. I had to count them at one point, which is why I know that number. I took my share and defended my share of expert depositions. I worked on appeals at various levels. So, I got to see cases fully.

I think today too few practicing attorneys and even fewer people in the electronic discovery space have had the advantage of that experience. As a result, we collectively spend far much more time and money on discovery activities than we should. And it's because we don't know when to stop. We don't know when we have enough data because we haven't been through that whole process. Adding that 16 years of experience has helped me better understand not just the extent of what potentially eDiscovery can do, but the value of appreciating the limits of what it should do.

Q: Electronic records have made the discovery process very costly and prompted changes to the federal rules to limit expenses and scope. Do you think they've had any meaningful impact?

A: Well, yes. However, there's a lot packed into that. First of all, as far as I have been able to determine, there aren't solid, reliable numbers available to back up any assertion there. What we do know is that the volume of data continues to expand enormously. We know that the volume of data available in litigation, pre-approved lawsuits, investigations, and the like is increasing. What we don't know is what the impact of things like the changes in the rules have had on it. I suspect the increases in discoverable data are like a Ferrari surging forward, and the changes in the regulations and efforts along those lines are like the brakes in a homemade go-cart. The single set of changes that have had the most impact are those concerning proportionality and sanctions.

Q: How do organizations use the emerging discipline of information governance to support their data strategies and projects?

A: I think in the world of IG, it's still a challenge. For a long-time, information governance was a practice, a methodology, an idea in search of a need. I can't tell you how many efforts I witnessed, corporate efforts that failed. They couldn't get funding because there was always something pressing. Whether it was taking the money to generate income or support a government investigation, to fight lawsuits, or for initiatives where you were forced to take some action, governance kept getting shoved to the back of the line.

What has changed over the last few years is the rise and tide of data privacy concerns driven by global legislation. That need to address privacy issues has opened up opportunities to get funding for information governance activities. If you get your electronic house in order, good things can flow. You can do a much better job of addressing your privacy needs and challenges. I think privacy is going to lead to some dramatic changes in the next one, two, and three years for information governance and electronic discovery, as well as in related areas. I think it's going to be very interesting and exciting times for those disciplines.

Q: These interviews touch on global management perspectives. I understand you spent some time with the Peace Corps. What did you learn from that experience that you've carried into your career?

A: The old marketing slogan for the Peace Corps was the toughest job you'll ever want. And I think that's the best one-line description of my experience. I got a level of responsibility at a young age that I could only have received in a limited number of ways. It was a lot of responsibility with very little structure or guidance. I was out in the middle of nowhere, a long way from any support systems, working with my local counterparts who were similarly situated. We had to figure out how to get things done ourselves and not count on support from anyone.

It was often a confusing and chaotic environment where the goals were very poorly defined. There was a lot of confusion. It sounds a lot like the world of electronic discovery, especially in its early days. So that was a part of the value. The more considerable value, though, is that it helped open my eyes to a better understanding that there is an enormous world out there. People approach things in different ways with different motivators, and at the same time, I recognized some commonalities.

I had to learn a completely different language, French, as well as enough of the local languages to do some basic navigation in the marketplace. It's not that different from having to figure out things like electronic discovery where there wasn't even a language when we started studying it. To try and understand cultural differences is kind of like figuring out the differences between how lawyers and how IT professionals approach things. Two different worlds that don't necessarily historically communicate with each other very effectively. But there are a lot of commonalities, and the best approach is just appreciating how big and complex the world is when combined with the possibility you might be able to make a difference.

Q: How did you choose this career? Or did this career choose you?

A: Several different things converged. My freshman year in high school, this was 1972, I took a course on computer programming, BASIC. In my sophomore year, I took one on Advanced BASIC, and I think Pascal. I spent much of my free time in high school writing code for the fun of it.

I went to college and had nothing to do with computers. Then I was a Peace Corps volunteer. Nothing to do with computers. I didn't even have electricity. But, coming back in 1983, I saw the IBM PC and realized that the world had changed while I was gone. Oh, man. Bought an Apple Macintosh the first month they were available for purchase. I took that with me to law school. I got frustrated with the very ethereal nature of law school and got involved at the first opportunity in the legal aid clinic.

In my second year, IBM donated a half dozen PCs to law school. The dean said, "I'm not sure what we can do with these in the classroom, but I think there's a place for them in the clinic." He gave them to the director who, in turn, looked at me and said, "You've got a computer. Go figure out what to do with these." I wrote a matter management system because there wasn't any PC networking in place yet. But it allowed us to manage our matters on those computers. Then I showed up at my first law firm, and they handed me a Dictaphone and said, "See how technologically advanced we are?" I thought, "What have I done to myself?"

So, I brought my computer into work, and two things happened. One, a steady stream of senior associates and junior partners came into my office, shut the door, sat down, and delivered the same message. It was "Lose the computer. Real attorneys do not type. You will never be taken seriously as a lawyer if you have a computer on your desk." Well, we know that's not how things played out.

At the same time, I got pulled into the largest set of cases the firm had ever handled, in part because I had that giant computer on my desk. We were going to have a million documents that were going to be coded, and that information was going into another computer somewhere. I had a computer, so there you go. I was put in charge. All of that eventually pulled me into the world of eDiscovery. I was just a few years in when our IT Director was hired away, and I was the functioning IT guy for a year and a half. After that, there was no escaping electronic discovery.

Chapter 10

Emerging from the Dense Digital Fog

Dr. Ulrich Kampffmeyer, Managing Director, Project Consult

Topics: Enterprise Content Management, Artificial Intelligence

"With AI looming ahead, we may even have to redefine what work is. Man is no longer the scale, the ruler, the canon."
Dr. Ulrich Kampffmeyer

Dr. Ulrich Kampffmeyer is the Managing Director of Project Consult in Hamburg, Germany, and a renowned expert on digital transformations, business intelligence, and enterprise content management. He holds a master's in archaeology and completed his Ph.D. in prehistory at the University of Göttingen.

Q: Ulrich, you write and teach about cultural and social changes in work environments that are a direct result of the emergence of digital transformations now that data is at everyone's fingertips. What change has the business world experienced?

A: The pace of digital transformation accelerates day by day. Cloud technologies, artificial intelligence, IoT, and other developments are happening so fast that there is a danger they'll get out of control. The mightier AI becomes, the larger the danger that it gets uncontrollable.

Consider Shoshana Zuboff, one of the first tenured women at Harvard Business School, and her three laws:

- Everything that can be automated will be automated.
- Everything that can be informated will be informated.
- Every digital application that can be used for surveillance

and control will be used for surveillance and control.

Neither our businesses nor society is currently prepared for those changes. Just have a look at the General Data Protection Regulation discussions on data protection as a general necessity, data safety as the requirement for continuity, data privacy by default, information governance to keep control, keep the value, keep information accessible, and so forth. These are basic requirements that should not be ignored like in the past. Future historians will call our era the dark age of the early information society.

Q: *You spent quite a bit of time at the Fraunhofer Institute, developing imaging systems and processes to support archaeological studies. Given that images provide so much of the fuel for artificial intelligence engines, do you envision some of our older legacy systems and indexes providing value to future AI efforts?*

A: In the mid-eighties, I worked on pattern recognition, image processing, database systems, and expert systems for archaeologists and prehistorians. Today, taking a computer, drones, and sensor systems to an excavation is standard. The capabilities of software, hardware, and self-learning algorithms are far more sophisticated than in those days. But let's consider so-called old-fashioned methods of organizing information. You mentioned the terms "legacy" and "indexes." Metadata is not legacy. It is a question of quality, control, and governance.

Controlled metadata, vocabularies and taxonomies are of special value to big data analytics, artificial intelligence, and machine learning. Controlled data sets work as guide poles to train new technologies with high-quality information. This is useful for automated indexing when capturing information, when sharpening enterprise search for qualified results, and managing your repositories with compliance requirements. Especially when it comes to compliance, straightly organized high-quality information is an asset. But, AI will change the game as well in the near future. Currently, classification schemes and file plans are developed manually by academic rules. In the future, software will analyze all information and organize itself by protection guidelines, user models, processes, value, retention.

Q: This series of interviews with global leaders in fields like information technology, risk, and compliance seeks to find common values and themes in these disciplines across disparate cultures. I know that you are an advocate of standardization. Are there any commonalities in the projects and people you've worked with that you believe should be universal goals?

A: Standardization is a necessity. Everywhere. We do it with our language, our terms, our grammar to enable understanding. We do it with hardware so that it supports interfaces and operating systems. We do it with software so that it can interact with other software and systems. We do this with the retention rules for documents in our records management systems. Standardization is everywhere; that's no question. The real question is, what has to be standardized and for which purpose? And is standardization something to prohibit innovation? Is standardization regarding streamlining and controlling data in opposition to the culture of a group of people or an organization?

The larger and more distributed an organization is, the harder the job of implementation of change and change culture. Old behavior, language barriers, time zones, cultural differences can sometimes make common values hard to define. Processes to keep values and make businesses run smoothly need, as well, a kind of standardization. This might all change in the future with artificial intelligence. Less work for humans means that human-driven use models and respect for human work will decrease. It's a major social challenge because people often define their status through their work. So, this is a common thread in all projects. Who is to redefine processes, keep workers involved, try to help them overcome their fears of losing their jobs, and be responsible for implanting a new mindset for a new type of work environment? With AI looming ahead, we may even have to redefine what work is. Man is no longer the scale, the ruler, the canon.

Q: In being at the forefront of enterprise content management (ECM) and systems design, you learned plenty of lessons about development. We live in a far more regulated environment than existed 30 years ago. Our challenges today intersect with privacy and security. What are the types of risks and concerns you believe developers of content management systems should be thinking about when building the next Documentum, SharePoint, Alfresco, or Relativity?

A: There is no future for old dinosaur architectures and big enterprise solutions. Modern solutions have to care for every type and technical format of information available. The basic strategy for products is automation. Not only to get rid of human work and to speed it up but to improve quality control and establish new areas of business opportunity. Integration is still a major issue. We are no longer talking about traditional records management systems for records managers but the integration of ECM functionality into other software. Interfacing and application programming interfaces (APIs) are crucial. And like the world of mobile apps, we will see services come up, which integrate and configure automatically into other environments.

Complex systems will only be manageable by AI-based administration software. So not only end-user relevant processes will be transformed but also the configuration, administration, and management of these solutions. The IT services concept will make sure that ECM functionality is available in the same way as Software-as-a-Service, Platform-as-a-Service, and on-premise. A change will be that end-users no longer see an ECM client because the functionality is integrated into the standard desktop environment. ECM loses visibility on the desktop and becomes standard infrastructure. All of these developments change the paradigm of the traditional ECM software architecture and functionality. They require new dev-ops, new development tools, listening to the user, faster testing and roll-out, easier configuration, pre-configured business solutions, and easy to use end-user interfaces. It's a big challenge for all companies developing any type of software.

Q: *There has been a lot of noise around the General Data Protection Requirement ((GDPR) specifically the "right to be forgotten" and stringent privacy and data retention safeguards, but we haven't seen much intellectual discussion around the broader social benefits the law intends to support. How do you see this "return to privacy" improving society when it seems that much of the younger generation not only dismiss the value of privacy but, as Simon Sinek has noted, see themselves through the lens of the over-sharing social media community?*

A: The GDPR has been in place for some time and is only now being enforced. It is not a return to privacy. Privacy requirements and regulations always have been here. But nobody really cared. We were careless with information and information sharing. And now we are complaining that internet giants are using our data. The new quality of the GDPR is twofold: on the one hand, it is for all of Europe and organizations dealing with European personal data and transacting business in Europe. So, it intends to become a worldwide standard. On the other hand, it threatens high fines for infringement.

This is a tool for enforcement we missed in the past, and that's why everybody started to care about it. But the other side is this, small businesses, associations, and others may come under threat of the GDPR. Where big companies can hire teams of lawyers and establish a data protection regiment, small businesses are overwhelmed by bureaucracy. Information management software is a necessary tool for larger companies to manage all data. They need the equivalent of a data map to identify what information is stored and it's quality, value, and legal character plus how it is processed. Smaller businesses struggle with these requirements because of their size, larger business because of the complexity and the sheer amount of data involved.

The social communities have a different view on the requirements. On the one hand, they have to care more about privacy. They must be able to deliver reports where they store data and what they do with it. On the other hand, the GDPR strengthens them because small forums, blogs, communities, groups, and businesses give up on complying and move their communities to Facebook, LinkedIn, or somewhere else. Communities like Facebook even use the necessary declaration of agreement to implement new technology like face recognition, which inflicts directly with privacy.

Privacy by design and privacy by default will be significant concepts of the future information society. But in reality, people choose the lazy options, and we don't invest serious efforts into the future of our information society. We leave this to science fiction authors and films, to CEOs of internet companies, and politicians. Privacy is not only about rights but obligations as well. These obligations tangle not only companies and public administrations. They apply to everybody of us, you and me.

Everybody has to take care of his own data and to respect the data privacy of all others. We cannot claim any right of being forgotten when we actively upload our directory of addresses to a social platform. In my opinion, data privacy and privacy rights is primarily a task for education, which has to start even before school. It is a task for developing a mindset about the value and the risks of information. Data Privacy has to begin in our heads.

Q: Predictive coding was introduced almost two decades ago, and while the technology has advanced, the barrier to adoption is still cost and complexity. Will advances in artificial intelligence and machine learning help make these tools accessible to smaller firms?

A: First of all, we have crossed the magic border of AI. AI is now not only self-learning and self-optimizing but like evolution, self-replication, and self-expanding. An example is the "Neural Network Quine." AI software is programming AI software, and AI software is managing AI environments controlled by AI administration tools. Machine learning will be standard in this new virtual world. This AI is different from our traditional perception of intelligence. It goes its own ways, inventing different methods, and is becoming transparent to human perception and intellect. It is here, waiting around the corner. We see a big war being fought by Amazon, Apple, Microsoft, Google, IBM, and others for the leadership role.

Today, AI is even free for end-users or comes with consumer products. The longer it learns, the more sophisticated it will become. AI will become part of every piece of software. The future of IoT with billions of devices will only be manageable by AI. Yes, it will become part of every cloud offering and will reach smaller firms. The only delaying factor is legacy software, legacy management, legacy behavior, legacy business models.

The overlapping, entailing, reverse-causing, accelerating innovation processes will encompass everybody. This is why I mentioned that our old ideas of information-driven society with well-informed citizens having control over information and machines would become overturned by dystopian models of a science fiction nature. Predictive analytics with artificial intelligence will play a role in our fight to keep control because software and systems will naturally anticipate what we will be doing better. Complete industries will change. First, those who deal with information only, like banks or insurances. Then manufacturing and others will follow.

Q: Based on your years of experience as a practitioner, lecturer, and consultant, what sage advice can you offer to a young person just entering the field of information management and information technology?

A: Well, education on information management is lagging behind the technology and information revolution. Learn to think by yourself, learn languages, learn how to communicate, learn methodologies, learn philosophy, learn to adopt change, learn not to stop learning throughout your life! Study something which is of real interest to you, what you love, which gives you intellectual satisfaction.

Chapter 11

Marketing Moving Targets of the Digital Revolution

Dux Raymond Sy, Chief Marketing Officer, AvePoint

Topics: Digital Transformation, Cloud Computing

"The two main challenges in digital marketing are time scarcity and white noise which seem more pronounced in the enterprise IT space."
Dux Raymond Sy

Dux Raymond Sy is the Chief Marketing Officer of AvePoint and is responsible for driving business and digital transformation initiatives for commercial, educational, and public sector organizations across the globe. He's also a Microsoft Regional Director and Most Valuable Professional and has authored numerous books, articles, and whitepapers on IT and business process strategy. He received his bachelor's in telecommunications engineering from Southern Polytechnic University.

Q: Dux, AvePoint specializes in leveraging the breadth of Microsoft technologies to help companies manage their cloud, on-premises, and hybrid environments. Some trends indicate at least a few enterprises have shifted back toward hybrid stacks after overextending themselves in the cloud. Will most enterprises eventually evolve from on-premises or hybrid infrastructures, or could factors such as data protection prevent total cloud adoption for some?

A: When it comes to enterprise technology, we rarely move backward. The cloud's cost, scale, efficiency access, and yes, even security advantages, are too desirable for on-premises or hybrid infrastructures to prevail long-term. What I will say is that the transformation will take much longer than the advertising of cloud providers would have you believe.

Surprisingly, most organizations are still not all in on the cloud yet. We did a study a couple of years ago that showed about 70 percent of organizations were still in hybrid architectures. We also sponsored a study with the Association for Intelligent Information Management (AIIM) this year that showed one in three organizations is maintaining at least two versions of SharePoint. Attitudes towards the cloud have changed, but now the conversation has turned to how to get there rather than why. Lastly, there are capabilities that the cloud offers that cannot be delivered on-premises. Cloud-based advanced services, like machine learning, artificial intelligence, and data analytics, open new opportunities for technical teams to drive business value.

Q: How is Infrastructure, Platform, and Software-as-a-Service changing the organizational hierarchy of IT departments, reporting structures, and collaborative teams? Are companies beginning to hire more administrators and get along with fewer developers, architects, and support staff? Where will the best IT jobs be in the next few years at the current pace?

A: What we have found is that people and organizations evolve slower than technology. Right now, most organizations are just shifting on-premises roles to the cloud. So, if you were the SharePoint or the Exchange administrator, you are now the SharePoint Online or Exchange Online administrator. But what about applications that don't exist on-premises? Who owns PowerApps? This strategy ignores the advanced workloads and connections between apps that exist in the cloud. What you do in Microsoft Teams impacts your exchange and vice versa.

What organizations need, and we haven't seen yet, are administrators that truly own the platform and look at platform-wide issues. If we see some of these issues just within Office 365, imagine what we will see as multi-cloud architectures become more popular. The best IT jobs in the next few years will be business enablers who have a love of learning. You will need to be agile in the era of tech intensity.

Q: What are some of the challenges in marketing IT services and products in a rapidly shifting digital landscape, and exactly how does the Chief Marketing Officer role in an IT company differ from one tasked with promoting traditional goods and services?

A: The two main challenges in digital marketing are time scarcity and white noise, which seem more pronounced in the enterprise IT space. The IT department is being asked to do more with less, and they only have so much time to lift their heads from their daily tasks to evaluate the bigger landscape and engage strategically with different solutions. So, you have to maximize the time and attention you do have. We try to have a good mix of different content for people to engage with, but we always try to be engaging and informative. We will have a 60-second video of me on LinkedIn eating Ramen and talking about digital transformation, but we will also do the 60-minute-deep dive webinar on customer challenges related to, but not centered on, our solutions. Every piece of content must have entertainment or education value, or it's a waste of time for our audience.

The other challenge in our industry is white noise. Not only are there a ton of vendors, but they are all making claims, some more valid than others. On top of that, since technology is often new and evolving, all the vendors are defining it or categorizing what they do slightly differently. It's so essential to build and maintain your credibility and invest time in educating your audience even when it doesn't directly relate to selling your audience. That's why we put a lot of resources into maintaining one of the highest quality blogs on Office 365, SharePoint, and digital transformation.

Q: Are artificial intelligence and machine learning disrupting our traditional enterprise content management (ECM) systems and strategies, and what steps can business leaders take now to be prepared for automated document lifecycle management future?

A: AI and machine learning have been impacting enterprise content management systems in mostly positive ways. One of the highest value use cases has been search. For example, Office 365 is getting so good at knowing what document I want to look at or edit based on my past behaviors. It's almost scary. Ultimately this is a good thing because there are a lot of industry studies that show employees waste too much productivity searching for content. However, we have seen nightmare situations where organizations haven't tagged or classified their content appropriately, and payroll data accidentally gets surfaced to the entire company. Ultimately enhanced search and AI is good, but organizations still need to be vigilant about their data.

We are seeing robotics being deployed within the enterprise to help enhance productivity. AvePoint launched AVA, a virtual assistant chatbot within Microsoft Teams, that allows end-users to restore their deleted or lost items in Office 365. This helps end-users get what they need quickly and removes some of the tedious tasks that IT admins have typically had to handle.

Q: Data protection has always been an issue with cloud technology, especially now with the General Data Protection Regulation and consumer rights laws in the United States. How do you prepare clients for highly technical cybersecurity and privacy challenges when so much of their data is in the hands of vendors and third parties?

A: AvePoint was named a strong leader in a recent Forrester Wave on GDPR solutions, so we help in a lot of ways. First, you mentioned so much data being held in the hands of vendors and third parties, and this is true. It's a risk that organizations must mitigate, but it's a risk that the industry has been aware of for a few years now. That means things like cloud security assessments for SaaS vendors have become standard, but they are still trapped in email and spreadsheet hell. We offer an enterprise risk management solution that helps automate this process and allows organizations to calculate their privacy and security risk as well as map their data flows across their organization and with third parties.

Second, you noted the challenge of data going to third parties, but the reality is the biggest challenge organizations have with their data is internal. A majority of organizations aren't classifying or tagging their data! How can they protect their sensitive data if they don't know where it is? This is a colossal compliance risk. We offer a data validation and classification solution that can scan structured and unstructured data across file shares and content systems to help organizations classify their data.

The third way we help organizations with data protection is by offering a data classification and protection solution that can identify and help resolve incidents in real-time and prevent people from uploading sensitive content to places they shouldn't.

Q: *We're conducting these interviews to elucidate global perspectives from leaders with diverse backgrounds and across industries. In reviewing your work, I came across some business lessons you learned on a big trip to Kamala, Uganda, where you facilitated a web development course for impoverished students. Can you tell me how traveling around the world has informed your perspectives on how data should be governed, and what if anything we can learn from science, technology, engineering, and math (STEM) students in the developing world?*

A: What we can learn from STEM students in the developing world is first to be grateful for the tremendous opportunities we have been given, and it made me realize that as such, we have a responsibility to impart this opportunity with those less fortunate. But also, on a personal level, the pure joy in being able to learn new things and to have a passion for your vocation is one of the things that get you out of bed in the morning.

Chapter 12

Illuminating the Physical Realm of Dark Data

Markus Lindelow, Principal, Iron Mountain
Topics: Analytics, Records Management

"Companies know the vast repositories of data they generate and store are valuable, but extracting that value is difficult. With classification tools using machine learning and applying policy expertise, we can shine some light on dark data."
Markus Lindelow

Markus Lindelow leads the Information Governance and Content Classification Practice Group for Iron Mountain, the world's largest information management company, where he's been pioneering breakthrough analytic techniques for over a decade. He holds a master's in computer information systems from Saint Edwards University.

Q: Markus, you work with companies to help them better understand and address decades of often-incomplete metadata tied to some of their most treasured information assets in the form of historical paper records and materials. In certain cases, your client's institutional memory has been completely lost. They're struggling to figure out whether to dispose of their records by balancing retention costs untimely destruction risks. How does your team leverage diagnostic, predictive, and prescriptive analytics to make sense of the data to make informed decisions?

A: Our content classification process focuses on making the best use of the available metadata. This means classifying records with meaningful metadata as well as analyzing the classified inventory to create classification rules for records with little or no metadata. We have identified attributes within the data that tend to correlate with classification conclusions. We assess the classified records associated with an attribute to create a profile that may inform a rule to classify the unclassified records sharing that same attribute.

If, for example, there are 100 cartons associated with pickup order XYZ, and 90 of those cartons have been classified, and furthermore, all 90 are classified to ABC100, can we create a rule to classify to ABC100 the ten unclassified cartons belonging to order XYZ? Clients then may weigh the risk when applying this type of classification rule, and the process may even include a random sampling of cartons for physical inspection to verify the classification.

Q: There's usually a disconnect between information managers and the legislators setting records retention periods. Over the years, strategies like "big buckets" have attempted to mitigate this obstacle, but they're imperfect and carry their own risks. What can be done to bridge the divide better?

A: There are two pieces to the puzzle of records management: classification and retention. A records retention schedule needs to be straightforward enough to implement so that users can apply record codes to records. But the retention periods for the record classes need to be specific enough so that some types of records are not over or under-retained because they are mistakenly grouped with others.

It is a balancing act, and big buckets can only be taken so far. If a record class contains record types that users or legal requirements suggest should have a different retention period, then a new record class should be created. The other area in which the business can affect retention is a prudent implementation of the retention schedule into the records management system. For example, a record class may be defined as event-based in the retention schedule, but if it is known that all records for that record class are sent to storage only after the trigger event has occurred, then the storage date can be used as the base date to calculate retention. Classifying records is only part of the puzzle. This becomes all too familiar for clients with a lot of active records in offsite storage. These records need to be reviewed periodically to identify records whose event triggers have transpired.

Q: *Why not keep everything forever?*

A: The keep-everything culture has evolved as a byproduct of cumbersome retention periods and reduced storage costs. Rather than make the tough decisions about particular data sets, records are often tagged with an overly conservative retention period. This leads to an ever-increasing repository of data that becomes difficult to access and analyze, as well as increased exposure to potential litigation. It's important to identify and remove ROT (redundant, obsolete, and trivial information) and retire or archive applications promptly. Collection, classification, and retention processes should be assessed and optimized. Collect only the minimum data required for a task. Build a manageable records classification scheme so that it is straightforward for users to apply a record code. Prudently implement the retention schedule and review retention periods periodically. These are becoming requirements in the modern era.

Q: *How are multinationals like Iron Mountain leveraging artificial intelligence techniques and machine learning to help clients measure and monetize their information assets?*

A: Companies know the vast repositories of data they generate and store are valuable, but extracting that value is difficult. Iron Mountain has entered into a partnership with Google Cloud to analyze unstructured data. The Iron Mountain InSight solution combines Iron Mountain's experience in data analytics and information governance with Google's artificial intelligence and machine learning capabilities. Iron Mountain is also working with MicroFocus and Active Navigation to offer content analytics. With classification using machine learning and retention applied using Iron Mountain's privacy and policy expertise, these partnerships hope to shine some light on dark data.

Q: You're a big supporter of your local math pentathlon and youth academics. What guidance do you have for a young person just getting started in preparing for a career in big data, consulting and analytics, or even an individual re-entering the workforce seeking opportunities in this developing field of technology and business?

A: Math and logic games are a fun way for children to start learning critical thinking in a competitive but supportive environment. With the preponderance of screens in children's lives, a productive way to channel this interest is through beginner programming classes. For example, the Scratch programming language created by MIT is a visual way to learn by programming with code blocks. If a child is attached to her iPad, an app called Swift Playgrounds can help her learn Apple's Swift programming language. Programming requires logic, patience, and focus. At its heart, programming is problem-solving, and running code to perform a function is very satisfying. Programming is becoming a second language and a pivotal tool for young people entering the workforce. An understanding of database design and development is also helpful to understand how information is organized and accessed.

Chapter 13

Navigating the Global Digital Economy

April Dmytrenko, Business Advisor, Information Governance & Compliance Strategies

Topics: Records Management, Compliance, Privacy

"Simple always wins over complex, and this is certainly key in consideration of the end-user and expediting goals."
April Dmytrenko

April Dmytrenko, CRM, FAI, is a pioneer in the fields of records management, compliance, and privacy. She works closely with diverse enterprises on developing legally compliant programs and building strategic partnerships between their internal and external teams. She serves on industry action committees and is an active speaker, trainer, and author. She earned her bachelor's in business administration and technology from California State University, Fullerton.

Q: April, years ago, you accurately predicted that privacy would be the next big frontier for individuals managing data processes and where so many of the jobs would be. We now have several legislatures drafting regulations, and Chief Privacy Officer positions can't be filled quickly enough. Is there still time to enter this emerging field and make an impact?

A: Right now, we are experiencing a fantastic transformation of the business environment but particularly the evolution of technology and the global digital economy. It is indeed an exciting time, but we are acutely (headline news) aware of the impacts of compromised data security and privacy, including the financial impact on brand and reputation, litigation, and the overall burden and distraction on the business. The exponential growth rate of incidents of data theft, damage, loss or inadvertent disclosure continues to expand not only in frequency but the scope, and complexity. While privacy concerns gained attention over 100 years ago and became topical again about 15 years ago, it is still truly in an infancy state. Privacy offers IG professionals a rich opportunity to expand their leadership or advisory role in maturing a unified approach to protection, compliance with laws and regulations, and incident response and recovery.

Q: In your role as a fellow of ARMA International, a premier organization for records management professionals, you've helped to connect organizations with practitioners who can demonstrate the benefits of information governance (IG).What steps do you think organizations like ARMA will play as managing data becomes such a ubiquitous responsibility?

A: A number of the core professional organizations have been dealing with an identity crisis for some time, and still struggle to have a clear and concise "elevator speech" on mission and value. Information governance, while it has a wide breadth, still has the industry confused, and remains a term that does not universally resonate with senior managers. The industry's professional associations, while they have tremendous value and passionate support, are challenged to maintain their position in a fast-evolving and complex field.

We are seeing the technology vendor market taking over a leadership role, and they may serve as the new defining force in setting direction and guiding the industry. Self-serving, yes, but it could be what is needed going forward. I am not concerned about relevance as it will continue to be all about information and technology, and the management, protection and leveraging of data as an asset. While the role of a traditional Records Manager may not continue to be relevant, I don't find it particularly concerning. The relevance is in the work, and it evolves.

Q: This book is tasked with identifying the common threads of wisdom woven throughout all the information management disciplines. Having worked in various industries as both a practitioner and a consultant, what principals do you see as key to successful outcomes in the management of data, technology, and people?

A: What I prefer to integrate with my approach is the KISS principle, or keeping it simple, and that includes when identifying a solution, selecting technology, developing taxonomy, writing policy, or planning the roll-out of better practices. Simple always wins over complex, and this is undoubtedly key in consideration of the end-user and expediting goals. This principle of keeping it simple does not mean time was not invested, analytics were not employed, or strategy was not used in gaining support, or implementing change. Intrinsic is being smart in maximizing simplicity in accomplishing your goals. To quote Albert Einstein: "Everything should be made as simple as possible, but not simpler," and da Vinci, "Simplicity is the ultimate sophistication."

Q: What is the most constructive lesson you've picked up as a practitioner that you were able to transfer into the business of consulting?

A: The importance of being able to connect with my organization's decision makers in a way that was meaningful to them and the organizations. As records management requires an enterprise-wide approach, I developed an instinct for understanding and aligning it with the overarching business goals. And like any business manager, I recognized I needed to be savvy in getting sustained support and budget for my initiatives. All my peers were after the same, and my area has long been considered an overhead operation that is far from being mission-critical. Of course, I disagree as I know what we do supports the bottom line.

What I brought to consulting was the keen understanding of the practitioner's challenges and helping them to reinforce and even elevate their needs for creating importance. Having sat on their side of the conference room table, I sometimes know what the right next step is might not align with right now for senior management or the organization. Initiatives may have a best practice order for executing, but it is better to get support for some now and prove value than to have no support. I respect the practitioner and strive to ensure they end up in a better place, feeling empowered going forward.

Q: Of the five major emerging areas, big data, blockchain, IoT, quantum computing, and artificial intelligence, which do you think will require the most attention from records management and information technology leaders and why?

A: What I think requires the most attention from IG and IT leaders is not related to any one area but having the ability to stop and invest the time, without impeding progress, on a strategic vision and path.

Too many organizations have a reactive rather than a proactive approach regardless of technology and emerging areas. As a result, continual "budget-year" investments can be made based on limited view aspects, frequently without much involvement by the business groups or consideration of where the business, as a whole, is headed. The precedence-norm of fast decision making over smart is compromising organizations in a variety of profound ways, including a chaotic information environment. Part of the vision needs to include managing the growing volume of content while maximizing its asset value. Otherwise, organizations will always be reacting and encumbered by addressing past investments and splintered tools supporting siloed groups.

Q: How did you find yourself gravitating towards the world of Records and Information Management?

A: The field found me early in my career, and it was a natural path. I have always been a very organized and analytical person intrigued by the enterprise-wide scope and value and viewed records and information as an organization's most critical assets. The application of technology to streamline manual processes was captivating. So, I gravitated and then made a career of it, having been extremely fortunate to connect with industry leaders who mentored my development and pushed my thinking.

Part III Relationships Matter

"You can take my factories, burn up my buildings, but give me my people and I'll build the business right back again."
Henry Ford

The innovative business minds that have shared their experience and advice in these pages have also been instrumental in developing and refining best practices and approaches in their fields, including big data, enterprise content management, blockchain, AI, privacy, IoT, and more. They are our wise mentors and friends. In our careers, we've been lucky enough to work closely with many of them to achieve common goals. Enjoying and being enriched by professional relationships is above and beyond the greatest gift you can give your career. Relationship building is, has always been and will always be, the most seminal skill and strategy we should practice and master.

As working professionals in the Information Age, we must strive to recognize and even anticipate emerging trends. Seizing upon those opportunities is possible when we choose to partner with change agents who share our vision and can work with us to transform our enterprises. We must reach beyond our teams or spheres of influence and work closely with the legal, regulatory, and ethical communities that study, measure, and moderate the impact of our technology and products on our respective fields. We need to plan and develop ourselves with a deep respect for the world that our products and services impact.

Today's uptick in cross-functional collaboration, particularly in the planning and review phases, is being driven by an explosion of regulations and laws passed in the EU, the United States, and across the world. While in part burdensome, it's also a catalyst for a new synergy we see across once siloed areas of our businesses. It is leading to a holistic approach to management, governance, and profits. The new demands of the digital economy and its ethical considerations like privacy and the environment are moving us toward a dynamic view of customer relationships and customer experience.

Relationships are at the core of business ethics and information governance (IG). There are various definitions of IG, but all seem to articulate and frame an end-to-end solution that leverages the best minds available to an organization to ensure decisions about digital information and its governance are not made in a vacuum. IG helps organizations consider all angles to ensure its long-term benefit on the organization as a whole is lasting, ethical, and risk-averse.

Information governance is unique in its collaborative benefit because its primary focus is data. Its ultimate impact on our bottom lines requires intelligent discussions and decisions about dynamic initiatives, policies, and custodianship. IG decisions today can easily make or break a company in the Information Age.

Consider the demonstrable catastrophic effects of a data breach or ransomware attack. That immediate threat is why the relationships between stakeholders on an IG team must remain candid, respectful, and informed. An impulsive decision or misdirected motive can end up exposing a vulnerability in the system or much worse. What makes a successful information governance team or program? You can have a solid roadmap and the best tools, but it's all dead in the water unless you have good relationships that bond your team.

Hail to the Chieftains

The analogy of corporate teamwork to that of professional sports is worthy of application in the context of information governance. In 1952, the little known but highly accomplished Seattle Chieftains college basketball team exemplified teamwork during an era of tremendous social change.

It's a shame that the fabled sportswriter Mickey Gordon isn't around anymore to share his first-hand accounts of those players because he tells the story better than we ever could. But the gist is that people growing up back then felt the Chieftains represented the very best of America, and in some ways, the best of a country still stuck under the thumb of Jim Crow. The Seattle Chieftains were an unlikely band of brothers who defended each other on the paint and the road of life.

The secret was in their diversity. In the 1950's it was quite a big deal to have Catholics, Jews, Blacks and Caucasians all on the same team. Despite a poorly funded program and incredible competition, thanks to the relationships they developed with one another, the Chieftains made it to both the NCAA and the National Invitational Tournaments. Those successes may be a lifetime ago, but they're certainly not ancient history. The obstacles and challenges we all face as individuals and teams may be a little different now, but the best solutions remain very much like they were in 1952, baked in the perfect balance between individuality and unity. If we can see past the colors on our faces, we always find that we're still wearing the same jerseys.

That was the formula behind the Seattle Chieftains and the ingredients for effective information governance programs. It's about harnessing the power of working relationships in the Information Age. Staying in the position, but seeing past the material qualities of the individual gets you the right expertise and ultimately to the goal line.

Sourcing the knowledge, experience, and talent from each team member makes you virtually unstoppable. Highly successful sports teams like the Chieftains have proven, coordinating talent into a coherent, productive, sustainable strategy is the best way to win, and win consistently.

A new way to set the table

At Compliance and Privacy Partners, we work with highly

regulated, US-based companies that have lots of talented folks. They're subject to many laws from HIPAA to the CCPA to a multitude of tricky financial rules. However, our solutions are only as effective as the commitment of our client's stakeholders to their own efficiency and compliance goals. Successful digital and information governance transformations require capital investment and executive sponsorship, but above all, a culture that values relationships. Directives may come from the top, but as they cascade down through the organization, it's the relationships between managers that ultimately determine whether the direction is ultimately successful.

No matter where our position sits in the organization, we can always find opportunities to benefit both ourselves and our teams. Today's leaders understand that to make a difference in an increasingly crowded field they'll need to:

- **Build:** relationships with IT, risk, legal, compliance
- **Plant:** seeds and be the gardener, not the flower
- **Nurture:** the right talent to execute and maintain the vision

Strong leaders in the Information Age know how to build and encourage the right types of relationships for themselves and among their peers. We plant seeds, create synergy, and remember to nurture tomorrow's talent. It's one way of reminding ourselves that nobody is an island, and the ocean around us remains a boundless sea of opportunity.

Aligning people with policy and policy with technology
Information governance as a discipline has already proven its ROI to corporations around the globe by demonstrating the value of aligning policy pillars and best practices with state-of-the-art technology. As AI, IoT, and big data continue to evolve as both operational necessities and revenue streams, it becomes essential to apply governance. IG is also a young discipline being

exploited by some opportunistic vendors and consultants.

Our strongest recommendation for new practitioners of IG, no matter what specialty they come from, is "don't put the cart before the horse" when committing to transforming your organization. Spend enough time building relationships with the business. Develop your strategy in line with their business goals. Set the table with the right stakeholders and remember to align your policies with your people and your technology.

Don't burn too many bridges

The keyword in the adage that you can't make a lot of money without making a few enemies is few. Like my father, the basketball player, or that old soldier from New Mexico, my Mother never wanted to find herself in a new room with an old enemy. By treating everybody with dignity, she managed to avoid burning many bridges. And for every bridge she burned, she's probably built a hundred more. When a job, project, or a deal doesn't go your way, you must strive to take the high road and never make it personal. You never know what the future brings or if a relationship you recklessly dismissed in years past might be holding back the keys to a new opportunity.

Just a few more folks you should meet

Our last series of interviews in this collection illustrates how relationships are indispensable for a long and successful career in any era, but especially in the Information Age. We open with a briefing at the Department of Defense with information that may not be confidential but should certainly be taken to heart. We proceed to the doctor's office, where an informatics expert takes the temperature on the quality of data in the medical world. Our checkup complete we head to the library where one of the institution's fiercest advocates makes a case for supporting this public necessity. A civic leader and data protection steward in Los Angeles then picks up that baton and hands it to a compliance specialist from Brussels who shares his know-how on the regulatory institutions and individuals running them. Close to the finish, we crack open a studio vault with one of the most accomplished archivists in Hollywood before concluding with the practical perspectives of a recruiter looking to fill *Tomorrow's Jobs Today*.

Chapter 14

Defending Freedom with Information Management

Mark Patrick, Chief of Information Management, Joint Staff, US Department of Defense
Topics: Knowledge Management, Cybersecurity

"Public sector practitioners mingling with their private sector counterparts creates mutual benefit. Like-minded end-users collaborate. Customer-client relationships are formed. Lessons learned and best practices are shared."

Mark Patrick

Mark Patrick, CIP, leads the Joint Staff's Information Management Team at the United States Department of Defense in Washington, D.C. He is a recognized thought leader in digital transformation, intelligent information, and knowledge management. He earned his bachelor's in foreign affairs from the University of Virginia and his master's from Tufts University Fletcher School of Law and Diplomacy.

Q: Mark, you've served your country as a sailor, helicopter flight instructor, and now as a national security executive. What initially piqued your interest in a career in government, and why did you ultimately gravitate toward leadership roles in its knowledge management divisions?

A: I am the son of a career Air Force officer who went on to a second career in municipal government following his military service. So, I am following in my father's footsteps to a large degree. After attending the University of Virginia on a Naval Reserve Officer Training Corps (NROTC) scholarship, I enjoyed

21 years in the Navy, flying, doing various types of staff work, attending graduate school, living abroad and working with members of all the military services and with the interagency, allied military partners, and civilian members of allied ministries of defense.

While in the Navy, I served as the deputy to the civilian who led the Joint Staff's Information Management Division, from 2000-2002, here at the Pentagon, the position I now hold. During that period, that civil servant retired, and I acted as the division chief for a period of months. I was part of the selection committee that hired his replacement. It was during those couple of years I was exposed to workflow, records management, business process, business intelligence, decision support, and a number of information and knowledge management practices. I developed a keen awareness of how important these were to the business of the Joint Staff, and any large organization in general, whether public or private sector. It was exciting to do these things for an organization with such significance for our Armed Forces and the nation as a whole. The Chairman of the Joint Chiefs of Staff is the principal military advisor to the Secretary of Defense and the President. The Joint Staff is his staff.

When I retired from the Navy in 2007, the civilian leadership position in the Joint Staff's Information Management Division was vacant again, and I decided to apply for it. I was selected, and 12 years later, I'm still here. Like my father before me, government civil service seemed like a natural follow-up choice to my military career. Leadership in information and knowledge management in a national security environment felt like a continuation of what I did in the Navy, building on everything I'd learned, but also providing a continued path to grow in a field that I found fascinating. The only downside: no flying anymore. One year later, the iPhone came out, and our digital world seemed to speed up. The information world has continued to pique my interest as things have changed rapidly, so I've stuck with it.

By the way, flying crewed aircraft and conducting a complex military mission involving multiple ships, aircraft, and submarines is one big information and knowledge management exercise—with a little hand-eye coordination thrown in! There is a direct relationship to where I am now.

Q: *You're actively involved in groups like AIIM, the Association for Intelligent Information Management, and have sat on its Board of Directors. How does business and technology insight gleaned from private industry think tanks like AIIM influence information governance practitioners in the public sector?*

A: Information is information. Data is data. A business process is a business process. It doesn't matter whether it occurs in the public or private sector. The fact is that most private sector businesses are smaller and more nimble than large government bureaucracies. Because of this, changes in the business technology environment have occurred much more rapidly there than in the public sector. It seemed obvious to me that if I wanted to learn the best way forward for public sector information and knowledge practices, I needed to familiarize myself with the innovation happening in the private sector.

AIIM has been around since 1943. I found it soon after taking my civilian job via my local chapter, the National Capital Chapter. It was there I met a very experienced group of vendors, consultants, and other end users that had spent their entire careers in the information management space. They were able to teach me about the evolution of enterprise content management systems across businesses — the pharmaceutical industry, oil and gas, finance, etc. SharePoint was becoming a big deal, along with other systems and vendors. I shared with my AIIM colleagues what I was learning in my organization as well (nothing classified, of course!). As my personal and professional relationships with these AIIM members grew, I felt grateful and volunteered to serve on the chapter board. After some time, my peers encouraged me to apply for a director's position on AIIM's national board. I was nominated, selected, and began serving in 2014. Normally a three-year position, I continued as Treasurer, Vice-Chair, Chair, and now I'm in my sixth and final year of service as the Immediate Past Chair.

AIIM has been my network. I've worked closely with folks from Microsoft, Box, Nuxeo, Gartner, OpenText, Alfresco, state government CIOs, private consultants, to name a few. It has been invigorating and rewarding, and I've always found that what I learn from my AIIM colleagues has direct or indirect application in the public sector. People, process, technology, and information innovation is transferable.

As I've attended AIIM's annual conferences, there has always been a significant number of public sector attendees from across various levels of government. I'm clearly not the only one. Public sector practitioners mingling with their private sector counterparts creates mutual benefit. Like-minded end-users collaborate. Customer-client relationships are formed. Lessons learned and best practices are shared. Training is facilitated, and practitioners grow their skills and, consequently, their value to their organizations.

Q: The government is sometimes between a rock and a hard place in responding to Freedom of Information Act requests. What does the public need to understand about the burden these requests place on a bureaucracy?

A: I can speak from my experience with the Department of Defense information, especially here in the Washington, D.C., area. Most of our information includes mixed classified equities of multiple agencies, both sub-agencies within DOD— say Department of the Army, Defense Intelligence Agency, a particular combatant command like US Central Command, or US European Command for example; and information originated by non-DOD agencies like the Department of State or the Intelligence Community.

When a request to search for or review information comes into the OSD FOIA office, after they determine the request is legal, bona fide, etc., they then have to send it to all elements within the department that have equity to conduct reviews or searches. They may determine at that point that other non-DOD agencies need to review the information as well. Sometimes this isn't discovered initially, but the DOD sub-agency will come back with the recommendation that the material also be reviewed by one or more other agencies. Once all of the reviews are in, the OSD FOIA Office has to combine them, adjudicate them for consistency, etc. and then send out the consolidated reply to the requester. This can take time.

Within the Joint Staff, when we are given a case by the OSD FOIA office, we have to determine which sub-element of the staff has equity in the information so that it can be staffed by the correct Original Classification Authority. The work eventually will get from a FOIA caseworker into the hands of an action officer who has subject matter expertise to conduct the review or the search. Sometimes cases can be quite large and require considerable time to complete, and these action officers are doing them as a collateral duty. They have a "day job" that they also must do.

Sometimes there is controversy over some classified equities that may have to be worked through. All FOIA cases also will be reviewed by legal counsel's office. In CY 2018, my declassification branch completed over 1,600 cases involving either the FOIA or mandatory declassification reviews and security reviews that are subject to the Executive Order on Classified National Security Information (EO 13526). These types of reviews have different sponsor offices within the DOD. We track each request meticulously from receipt to return to the proper DOD office that interacts directly with the requester.

I take it as my duty as a civil servant to ensure that whatever should be released to the public is released—or rather that we recommend to the OSD FOIA Office that it be released. However, I also am determined that anything that is properly classified should be withheld, which is also in the best interest of our citizens and our young men and women in harm's way.

This case workload across the federal government continues to grow year to year as more and more of our citizens have discovered how easy it is to initiate requests from their home computers. Note one does not have to be a US citizen to use the FOIA. Not surprisingly, our human resources to work these cases have not kept pace, although we have increased the efficiency of this work by using electronic workflow tools and tracking. There are even private organizations that have built a business around helping individuals file FOIA cases. It is a hallmark of our democracy that these processes exist, but they are not free and to mismanage our properly protected national security information by incomplete processes would not only be illegal, it could end in tragedy. The resources required to do this work are always in competition with resources needed to do all the other things agencies must do. They are limited.

All of this is to say that what may appear like foot-dragging is really a patriotic attempt to serve both the public and our men and women in uniform. Could processes be improved? Always. Are some FOIA offices more efficient than others? Certainly. However, I am proud of the thousands and thousands of cases my division's declassification branch has worked over the last 12 years, and if FOIA requesters knew the details, I believe they would be most appreciative.

Q: Cybersecurity is an essential component of our national defense, and threats from foreign actors are becoming increasingly sophisticated. Yet federal, state, and local governments have limited resources to assist private entities investigating breaches and ransomware attacks. Where does a business's responsibility to protect its own IT infrastructure end and the government's role in defending it begin?

A: Fundamentally, it's about risk mitigation and resource management for businesses, governments, and individuals alike. Like many issues that have only recently come to be as technology has evolved rapidly in recent years, resolution may only come through testing in the courts, legislation, etc. This will take time. I expect there will ultimately be public/private partnerships that must emerge. US Cyber Command is very new, having acquired combatant command status this past May.

The public's awareness of these issues is mixed, and some of the risks will be assumed by citizens. The populace must learn to be responsible with their personal data. As awareness increases among the public, all levels of government, and within the private sector, and as the cybersecurity sector matures and grows, things should improve, but like our physical defense, our cyber defense will never be a 100 percent assured. The only way to ensure zero risk is to live in a cave and stay off the web. Not likely for most of us, and even for those who would choose such a lifestyle, they'd likely be picked up via satellite as they went about their off-the-grid foraging activities!

The government will have to balance the resources spent to mitigate cyber risk with the resources required for all the other required tasks it must perform. Companies and individuals will have to do the same. Engagement and collaboration between these three groups will be continuously necessary.

Q: Following the 9/11 terrorist acts, the U.S. took steps to ensure its security agencies were better equipped to share information and communicate. Besides leveraging technology to support interoperability, what have we done from a training perspective to promote better control over the handling of, and compliance with, confidential records and official systems?

A: I can only answer this question from my local perspective.

In short, a combination of training, automation, managed access to systems, and physical spaces are required. On the Joint Staff, training in the proper handling of classified or sensitive material is conducted during on-boarding for action officers. Refresher training is an annual requirement. As knowledge workers across the federal government create classified unstructured data, a human still must understand his/her agency's classified equities and know how to mark or tag electronic documents accordingly.

Automation can assist with minimizing human error, but there will always be a training requirement to ensure that documents and data are properly managed by the originator and anyone who handles information across the enterprise. If artificial intelligence and machine learning are used, a human will still be required to "teach" or configure the machine so it can detect sensitive information and prompt appropriate action.

If spillages occur, processes must be in place to mitigate associated risks, assess and respond to damage, and revise procedures to prevent future similar occurrences. Security clearance vetting processes are in place at the point of hire to try and prevent nefarious mishandling. Throughout a federal employee's time of service, continuous monitoring and/or periodic reviews of the individual's fitness for a security clearance are conducted.

With the rise of "need to share" over "need to know," the concomitant greater risk must be mitigated via system access controls, proper marking, and training. It will always be a balancing act when sensitive information must get to those who need it at "the speed of relevance."

Q: With deep fakes, AI inherent bias, and misinformation campaigns capable of drastically impacting the way citizens process information, what role if any does government have in combatting the disruptive social impacts they may have on the citizenry?

A: I believe government has a role, but the specifics are

complicated. There is some amount of "it depends" here. If another state or non-state actor is attempting to impact public opinion to affect a US election, this becomes a matter of national security at the federal level. State and municipal elections could be viewed differently. "Disruptive social impact" is somewhat vague, and I'd say government involvement should be considered on a case-by-case basis. Sowing the digital seeds of general social discord with the intent to create chaos, dysfunction, or further polarizing our society becomes tricky. It will need to be further analyzed, considered in the context of privacy laws, espionage laws, first amendment rights, and others. Legal precedents will need to be established in our courts, and perhaps legislation or national policies are required.

There are a number of novel legal issues at play with which government at all levels will need to contend. The digital commons, like international waters or space, can be leveraged for good or bad. International organizations may need to get involved, and the same sovereignty issues will come into play when those organizations address other issues. Coalitions of the willing have their limits. Governments at all levels can educate and work with their communities to raise awareness of the risks and mitigation strategies that should be considered.

Q: What's the best advice you can suggest for a person considering a role in knowledge management and seeing the military as an avenue towards that ultimate goal?

A: Entering the military for knowledge management or any specialty requires research first. All branches of the Armed Forces and the civil service are doing knowledge management in some capacity. But each of these services has its own culture and subcultures with which one should become familiarized before enlisting or pursuing an officer's commissioning program. Read military web sites, review USA Jobs, follow media in the knowledge and information management fields.

I believe that knowledge management, information and records management, information technology, cybersecurity, and data management are all different parts of the same information and data portfolio. More and more, collaboration among professionals that have these subspecialties will be paramount. You do none of these in a vacuum. In the end, this evolving workforce is serving the mission of the organization. What the organization's leadership needs is the just-in-time data and information to make decisions or achieve situational awareness.

I have often described these overlapping fields of expertise as analogous to instruments in an orchestra. Each instrument is needed, but the instrumentalists must not only master their individual skill, they must understand their fellow musicians and be able to play in such a way as to create harmonious, beautiful music. There should be a conductor who knows how to put them all together with the wave of a baton—and likely lots of practice. Without this synergy, the only thing produced will be a cacophony of tuning noise.

The military is only one way to get there, but folks must count the cost of military service. It's not for everyone. Note that both military members and federal civilians take similar oaths of office "to support and defend the constitution of the United States against all enemies, foreign and domestic." If that oath resonates, military service appeals. and one has a keen interest in information, data, and knowledge management, I'd say full speed ahead!

Chapter 15

Diagnosing the Healing Power of Informatics

Dr. Katrina Miller Parrish, Chief Quality Information Executive, L.A. Care Health Plan

Topics: Informatics, Compliance, Work-Life Balance

"The minute the patient walks in the door, you've got to let them tell their story. You can't assume by looking at a person or looking at the data that you know what's going on."
Dr. Katrina Miller Parrish

Dr. Katrina Miller Parrish is a physician, researcher, author, and Chief Quality and Information Executive for L.A. Care Health Plan. In her distinguished career, she has held leadership roles in prominent health organizations, received noted fellowships, and lectured at institutions, including USC's Keck School of Medicine. She received her bachelor's in biology from Reed College and MD from Eastern Virginia Medical School.

Q: Dr Miller Parrish a hotly contested provision in the 21st Century Cures Act aims to increase IT interoperability and information sharing amongst healthcare groups. Yet those rules have met pushback over privacy and security concerns. How do health organizations and executives manage regulatory pressures, and how do they impact a workforce's overall tactical capacity?

A: A health organization like ours is beholden to regulations. LA Care Health Plan is a public health entity, and we receive our authority directly from the State of California and the County of Los Angeles. That means while a board approves everything we do, it can also be reviewed by the LA City Council or the state.

Every day is spent making sure we're adhering to all of the rules. Those could even come from the federal government or a line of business serving the Medicaid population or perhaps Medi-Cal in California.

We're regularly audited by the Department of Healthcare Services (DHS), and so we have to adhere to regulations, or we wouldn't exist. During an audit, if they raise an issue, we'll get a finding and sometimes have to develop a corrective action plan for it. We can fix it, but we have to commit to a resolution that takes time. It affects our capacity, and in contrast to for-profit organizations and how fast they can move, we have a few more hoops to jump through.

It can take years to get initiatives to implementation because of all the necessary steps we have to take. I think part of working with a public health authority or a government entity is just knowing that's the case. You understand that you have certain requirements. Part of what my world is all about is figuring out how to go through all of those processes as quickly and efficiently as possible. Asking what can we do in parallel? What has to be contingent upon something previously done? Then trying to make it happen as quickly as possible.

Q: Does that imply you're in favor of legislation like the 21st Century Cures Act?

A: I'm in favor of interoperability as much as reasonably possible because, for us, we want to get as much data in our door as we can, especially for population health management. The more we get, the more we understand about our population, our members, and about our providers and network too. We're interested in having access to as much data as feasible. So basically, anything that comes along that safely decreases information blocking for a public health benefit, we can get behind.

Q: In the Affordable Care Act (ACA), the actual standards defining the Electronic Medical Record (EMR) were debated and delayed. How do you adapt to waiting for regulatory specifics? Do you drive forward with your technology initiatives and hope they're agile enough to adjust to the final regulations?

A: In our network, we work with eight different EMR's. The top five systems represent a majority of the population, but we have to try to figure out how we potentially work with the rest, which is why we lean on the health information exchanges. We work with three of those. It's still not enough, and we're very early in making that work. But what our "Health Information Ecosystem" strategy is partly about right now is working with whomever we can, getting as much good data in as we can for our population health purposes, and processing it efficiently and on time.

That takes a little initiative until you discover where your barriers are, and it hasn't been so much the regulatory barriers. It's technical barriers that challenge us. When we're talking about regulatory barriers, they have to do with the type of data. For example, when we're talking about mental health data, substance abuse data, there are some carve-outs that the state Medicaid programs will insist on treating and protecting differently.

The exchanges need to speak to each other, and they're getting there, but the ACA legislation didn't adequately address them, and that's been a challenge. If considerations had been put into the ACA in a meaningful way, we might be much further down the line, but they didn't make it about true interoperability, and they didn't give enough incentive to the vendors to do anything about it.

Q: Health informatics leverages AI and big data strategies to analyze health populations to improve overall outcomes, but the quality of the data sets used carries the potential to influence and produce unintended results. We already see inherent bias in other industries, but what's it mean for the medical world?

A: One of the things that we try to do, for example, in the case of claims, encounter, and population data, is to develop risk stratification or other adjustments. Because what we're trying to do is say, "This person or this group has a higher risk or higher severity of illness." Or, "Here is some potential for a higher cost. How can we address them differently than in a lower risk population?" So, yes, we do assign quality control resources and monitor those analytics to make sure we're understanding the data correctly.

All of our groups come to us frequently and say, "You're not calculating the risk adjustment or the risk stratification correctly. We think our population is higher risk than what you're representing." But there's not a lot we can do with that anecdotal response right now. All we can do is grab all the data we can find.

Of course, a lot of data isn't perfect. It may be a spectrum of corrupt to bad data entry. If we're talking about the kinds of codes that we'll get representing a claim or encounter, the quality of that data will vary. A claim is when you're asking for reimbursement for services, so it's a fee for service scenario, like an invoice. An encounter is when services are under a capitated payment where we're already paying that entity a monthly amount to take care of a certain number of people. We get data in the door about the services they received, but they've already been paid for it. Therefore, the incentive to send us good encounter data is far less than the claim data.

Q: As the quality assurance professional in your organization, even though you're primarily responsible for population health care, are you also possibly catching some fraud?

A: Yes, in some cases. We have a special investigations unit, SIU, and I'm the chair of the Credentialing and Peer Review

Committee. That's where we look at those kinds of issues, and we work very closely with our SIU unit. For example, when they identify providers who are just writing tons of prescriptions for one particular medication and we find out that these patients whose names are on the prescriptions never received them (and don't even have a diagnosis matching them), it raises a flag. We can identify them through algorithms, through data from payment integrity or our pharmacy data.

Q: Do you develop your systems and tools for this kind of data mining and analytics, or is there software already available?

A: It's a mix. There are software tools out there where you can do that first pass at running the data and finding trends, but I think that we still are learning how to set those algorithms up. It's another place where bias could come into play. We could identify the wrong people, and so we have to review the first pass of the data carefully. If it doesn't make sense, we try to confirm it. If we see a trend, we have to ask, "Okay, is there a good reason for that trend?" Let's say we have a provider identified for tons of prescriptions of one type, like risky or expensive, but then we go and find out that that's a neurologist who is dealing with kids with intractable epilepsy. Okay, well, then that makes good rational sense.

Q: Do you have to prioritize who you put under the microscope, especially with the SIU, because you can't go after every single problem or person?

A: Yes, and we have ten thousand providers! In this committee, we're focused on the providers' side of things a little bit more than the member side of the equation, but the numbers are so huge you have to use whatever is available. This is what we do with population management, as well. We've got to figure out what that spectrum is, then decide where to put resources.

Q: In response to technology's effect on litigation, most states require attorneys to demonstrate technical competence. With the growth of Informatics, do you expect medical professionals to be held to similar education requirements?

A: I hope so. I've got a family medicine background, but I also have a clinical informatics background, and there are maintenance certification requirements for both of them. Again, we're all working with EMRs, and if you have folks who could do so much better with that knowledge, even with just basic EMR wisdom, like knowing about pre-checked order sets or templates for notes or ways to find different orders, it would be advantageous.

Q: Would that type of education be as relevant for an oncologist as opposed to a podiatrist?

A: It depends. Everybody needs to have some level of experience to enter and pull information out of an EMR. There are some specific tricks to be able to do that well, and it's not just about how to make sure the information gets in appropriately. Successive folks are going to be seeing those patients and have to understand what happened to the patient. If you have a medical assistant or office staff, and they're trying to find a report on a patient, how easily can they get to that data, and in how many ways?

Q: We now have changes to board structures where Chief Information Security Officers are no longer reporting to a Chief Information Officer. They're going directly to the CEO because cybersecurity is so paramount. Is that now the case with medical organizations? Does the Chief Medical Information Officer sit in the boardroom?

A: Generally speaking, I think the C-Suite remains similar to what it has looked like for a while. In our case, we have a Chief Medical Officer, and then you have some others reporting up and transitioning all of the time. We have a Chief of Enterprise

Integration, and I'm Chief of Quality and Information. I think the reporting structure itself can be a little bit different sometimes depending on the organization and the people. If you have a COO who is better at overseeing some areas of medical operations, then it's appropriate for some of those administrative medical staff to report up through that person. It depends. The technology efforts that we have here are just ever-present and constantly changing, and of necessity must be as efficient and flexible as possible at all times. The reporting structure almost doesn't have to matter so much as long as you have the affected stakeholders making sure the right things are being done for projects and initiatives to succeed.

Q: So, what exactly made you choose the field of Informatics?

A: I went into Informatics because I liked the combination of clinical with data and with business. I think it's part of being a family physician. I like being able to have my hands in a lot of things and understanding a lot about data, which is the informatics side. I like having that variety. When I was doing family medicine, I felt like I could do way more than taking care of one person at a time. I loved my patients, and we had great relationships. I learned a lot, they learned a lot, but I really love population health because I can make an impact on millions of people with huge programs that can not only affect a community in Los Angeles but conceivably far beyond that.

Q: As a trained physician, you have a perspective on the stresses of data-driven life on the body and mind. Society is just beginning to understand the side effects of excessive dependence on our devices. How do we address infringements of technology on work-life balance?

A: I have a department of about 90 people, and I try to make sure they understand their priority is themselves, their second priority is their family, their third priority is work. I try to reiterate that all of the time for my department, and when it comes to individual people with their own issues, I try to make sure they're focused on the right things. They've got to have their priorities in order and believe if they come to me and have to take some days of PTO that I'm going to understand and put that before the demands of an audit.

Audits will happen; work will happen; L.A. Care will continue to exist. The most immediate thing is that these people take care of themselves and their families. Maybe that comes from me being a family physician or being a family person, but it's in there. It's ingrained in me that I need to make sure everybody knows that.

That said, I have to try to model the behavior. That part is not as easy. I do get complaints from colleagues that tell me I'm not always practicing what I preach. So, every day I too have to work on that. What time do I have to be at work? What time can I leave work? Do I need to be here seven to seven? Do I need to be the one taking care of editing and reviewing all of the documentation that comes in and out of my department? I want to do a little better with that, but I think it's a familiar challenge.

Q: We now have this concept of social media as a prism through which people begin to see themselves, where every person must have their brand. This is an incredible pressure that I don't think anybody ever expected. How is that affecting people's work life?

A: Well, millennials are a whole generation that has grown up with these devices attached to their hands, and even more so the later generation. One example of my own sort of experience with that was when I was on call. I had a beeper at the time, and I started to have a physiologic reaction to every time that sound would go off. You knew you were going to deliver a baby, or you had to go to the ICU or the ED, or something was going to be an intense situation to deal with. And what I progressed to is now I rarely, if ever, have my phone actually on a ring. I always have it on vibrate at this point. I don't pay attention to it sometimes. I put it away, and, in the evening time, I might not pay attention to it for the whole night.

You have to do what works for you. Some people are workaholics, and they want to work every day of the week. That's fine, but I do want to try to espouse and motivate for a better type of balance.

Q: You've achieved success in medicine, and now you're immersed in informatics and business optimization. How has your medical training informed your approach to solving the business piece of it?

A: I think first of all, in medicine, we learn to assess a situation, take in the data, try to figure out what a differential diagnosis would be. You're never trying to go right to a solution. You want to see what all of the possible solutions are in all relevant scenarios. I kind of think of differential diagnosis in a way, like a root cause analysis, where you're trying to look at all of the possibilities before you get to your final answer. And then, when you get to your top three, top two, or even the only one it could be, based on the data you have available, then you move into your solution. You could look at your solution as a project, as an initiative that follows a particular process.

We use the System Development Lifecycle process and others. And it's interesting how much my medical training set me up for being able to assess data in a way that falls in line with almost any kind of stepwise assessment.

Q: Your work has taken you from the L.A. marathon to as far as Tanzania. What's the best lesson you learned going out into those communities and abroad that you've been able to bring back into your work and professional life?

A: It's a simple answer, but it's to listen. And if we're talking about the Los Angeles marathon, you've got five seconds to listen to that person and see what their exact issue is and try to figure out what to do about it because they're running and they're going to come in for a few seconds, and you've got to get them out on the road again.

In Tanzania, it is so foreign to western allopathic medicine physicians as to what could be going on with a patient, that you've got to listen to what their story is to understand that, number one you may be looking at something like malaria or something unusual in the United States, but it could also be something totally different. For example, we had issues in one particular area where there was a myth that if you had AIDS and you had sex with a virgin that you would be cured. And so, we had to deal with that situation and those who truly believed. We had to listen and think about what we could do with the population there to try to redirect them to the right people who could change that perception. But we had to listen to those folks to understand where to focus our efforts.

That being said, with medical care, the minute the patient walks in the door, you've got to let them tell their story. You got to give them the time because you can't assume by looking at a person or looking at the data that you know what's going on. Not only that, you don't know what their priority is. If you're not working with them on their priorities, then they're not going to trust you in terms of how you're working with them.

The same thing is true in business. If I don't listen to what my direct boss, my CMO, is telling me about his preference or his opinion or priority, I'm going to go the wrong direction completely. I've got to listen to what he's saying, to listen to what the CEO is saying, and put it all together to make sure that I strike the right balance. The same thing can be said for my department. If I'm not listening to them and or understanding what their real issues are, then we could have problems in terms of employee engagement.

Chapter 16

Your New Neighborhood Library

Patrick Sweeney, Political Director, EveryLibrary
Topics: Public Affairs, Library Science

"When you think about the fact that libraries are about information and not simply about books, you begin to see where the value is."
Patrick Sweeney

Patrick Sweeney is the Political Director for EveryLibrary, the United States' first and only political action committee for libraries. He is co-author of *Winning Elections and Influencing Politicians for Library Funding* and *Before the Ballot: Building Support for Library Funding*. In 2019 he was named one of the "40 under 40" by the American Association of Political Consultants (AAPC). Patrick received his master's in library and information science from San Jose State University, where he now teaches courses on politics and libraries.

Q: Patrick, your advocacy work helps libraries become successful in securing funding, expanding influence within communities, and staying relevant in the digital age. With information at everybody's fingertips, how have librarian's challenges evolved, and why is supporting them so key to the health of our citizenry?

A: Well, when you think about the fact that libraries are about information and not simply about books, you begin to see where the value is. What it means is that people are visiting libraries and seeking much more complex information, and they're looking for guidance in navigating all of it. These are the same tasks that libraries performed when information was only found in books.

Librarians are helping people find the right websites to answer their questions, but there's also a ton of services. They're working closely with the public through informative and collaborative programming. For example, you can go to the library if you want to learn about starting your small business. You can attend one of their training programs or visit one of their business centers. You can find a lot of your information for starting your small business and how to navigate everything legally. So, the role of the library hasn't changed within society. It's just how we access information within the library that has changed.

Information isn't at everyone's fingertips. It's only at your fingertips if you can afford the cost of internet access at home or the cost of having a smartphone or a computer at home. We also have issues around connectivity through the major ISPs, which have monopolies in various cities. There are major connectivity issues in certain areas where the library is legitimately the only access to broadband internet for the community. In Alaska, where the connectivity issues are exceptionally challenging because of the geography or the terrain, libraries are adversely affected. It's also not cost-effective for Comcast or AT&T to run fiber networks out to these very small towns, and the library is often the only place that provides that essential service.

Q: How exactly are libraries and educational institutions today leveraging big data analytics to stay competitive in local, state, and federal political spheres?

A: They aren't for the most part, and that's one of the big issues. If we had better data and were able to use big data analytics in a more meaningful way, we'd have a better understanding of who supports libraries and why. That insight leads to an understanding of how to communicate with various demographics of the public. For example, how do we talk to conservatives about libraries? How do we speak to progressives about libraries? We have a lot of that data, but it has never been effectively utilized.

There's also a handful of underlying issues that come with that option. The biggest one that I can think of is the privacy discussion around using people's data. Libraries are radically supportive of privacy rights. You know, if you check out a book at a library, there's almost no way for anybody to find out what you checked out.

Q: I recall discussions during the drafting of the Patriot Act and specifically the controversy over whether the government should have access to who checked out books like "The Anarchist's Cookbook." Are you suggesting it remains a conflict of interest for the libraries?

A: Yes, but what does that do for us? That bleeds over to the way we market ourselves, the way that we use, and leverage big data and how we stay competitive. Because the use of that data encroaches on that privacy domain, right? If I have enough data about an individual to have a meaningful conversation with them about libraries, then depending on how I came across that data, I could violate any number of nuanced privacy rules and standards.

Libraries don't like keeping any data on their patrons. For example, there was a recent issue where Lynda.com sells its platform to libraries. To use Lynda.com through your library for free (you get access to all those pieces of training and courses with a library card), you have to get a LinkedIn account. And LinkedIn tracks which Lynda courses you access. Librarians are upset about the fact that kind of tracking occurs.

Not having that tracking option also means that LinkedIn can't target those people with marketing that could be beneficial to libraries. It also means that we don't have any data to target our users better, to talk to them about the things that they want to learn, or what they want to do in their library. Consider this scenario, "I don't know that you like science fiction books because we don't keep that kind of data, so how can I tell you about new science fiction books that just came in?" You see, libraries lose that marketing advantage and partially to their detriment. But on the other hand, it's such a core belief of librarianship that it becomes difficult to rationalize.

Q: Are you concerned that new data privacy laws might make it cumbersome to connect with audiences, not just in libraries but in non-profit spaces or for political advocacy?

A: There's a couple of things that come to mind. Cambridge Analytica, for example, was a fascinating scandal because they weren't doing anything different than what anyone else was doing, building data sets around individual voters. It's just that their process for getting that data wasn't exactly ethical to put it lightly. Those same types of data sets are being built by the DNC, the RNC, and others. Everybody in politics builds out the same data sets.

The interesting thing is that the whole thing blew up and underscored the need for the GDPR. In the UK, we just launched a national advocacy project with the Charter Institute of Librarian Professionals, the professional association for librarians. We have to comply with all of those kinds of rules.

At first, I was concerned about the GDPR being implemented, but what we see in the nonprofit base is that these businesses and political organizations are now managing their data in a much more productive and efficient way. They're becoming effective at rallying support for their causes, simply because the GDPR mandates the kind of data maintenance they should have been doing all along.

One example is that they were buying bulk email lists, and you can't just buy email lists like that anymore. You can't just purchase user sets. Ironically, the return on those kinds of purchases and those kinds of spends is so minute that it's not even worth it. It's far more efficient, and you get a much higher ROI if you spend your money cultivating opt-ins instead of purchasing lists. So, it does make it more cumbersome, because you have to do more strategy. You can't just click a button and have half-a-million people to send an email to. You have to think about how to engage these people. How do I get them to opt-in? How do I get them to want to find out about this campaign? By thinking about all of those considerations, we become far better at raising both money and awareness.

Q: *What about the financial burden imposed by data protection and privacy requirements?*

A: I imagine if you had a list of ten million people to comb through, it would be expensive. But if you're building from scratch, or you have a couple of thousand people in your database, it probably isn't too tricky. I think almost all the platforms that I know of today that operate with GDPR in mind already have those processes built-in. People opt-out, and the platform does most of it all automatically. You don't have to worry about long hours maintaining this data.

Q: *With the advent of the internet and the surveillance state, are libraries still on the front lines of defending privacy and censorship? How do they manage to be a nonpartisan resource in the modern era?*

A: Libraries have historically been committed to privacy and ensured none of your records are accessible. If you check out a book, there is an electronic record while you have it, but once you return it, all that tracking activity is removed from the record in all ways, shapes, and forms. Nobody can ever find out what you checked out after the fact. You can't even go back to your library and say, "Look, I checked out a book last year. What book was it?" They won't be able to tell you just because they don't retain any of that data.

We have a lot of discussions around this kind of stuff. What if somebody gets on a library computer and looks up how to do something malicious? How or do we even begin to protect against something like that? Where's the line in the sand? Right now, for example, there's a big discussion around viewing adult material in libraries.

In terms of browser history, there's a lot of discussion around adding filters to the computers and whether libraries be involved. Because those filters also might block out some legitimate searches. Should we trust our fellow citizens enough to allow them to access the internet as if they would at home, without tracking anything like we do when they check out a book?

Q: Has the ease of conducting academic library research, by relying too heavily on search engines, had any negative impact on the quality of the results? Do you think by substituting or supplanting search results for traditional library science and peer review, we're possibly producing data that tells us what we want to hear rather than what we should know?

A: I'm not entirely sure that we're seeing the impact of all this as much as we will in the next ten years. The big issue is that Google provides those search results without much context. What that leads to is a situation where I can right now prove just about any silly idea I have in my head through a Google search. If you're looking at flat-earthers, you're looking at anti-vaxxers, you're looking at 9/11 being an inside job, you know those results erroneously validate those conspiracies.

Q: Does that mean there is there going to be further regulation of content? What are some of the solutions? Do we de-anonymize the internet?

A: This is one of the central issues in the recent election meddling controversy. Anybody can pretend they are a citizen of a different country online and then do whatever destructive thing they want to do. I don't know if de-anonymizing the internet is the right solution, but I do think that as we normalize what people are calling research, which is equivalent to referencing a couple of videos that you agree with on YouTube, as that becomes normalized, it absolutely might filter into academia. It could start filtering into dissertations and legitimate research as a regular part of academic research. Another example, and one of the things that we keep hearing in libraries, is the falsehood that states determine the future prison population by measuring third-grade literacy levels. And to some that may sound "truthy," but no state does that.

We see the same thing with online books that misattribute facts to the wrong person. We know that it finds its way to book publishing because now you can do self-publishing. They're sold on Amazon. Publishers are getting desperate for increasing revenue because book sales have slumped. They've been picking back up again, but they declined for a while. When you see an economic weakness, such as slumping book sales, and you want to turn that around, you're maybe prone to publishing things people want to hear rather than the truth.

We just had a controversy like this in our libraries only a couple of years ago. There was a famous doctor who Oprah had had on her show. He wrote a book about holistic medicine. It turned out that several of his cures for various diseases were dangerous. So even libraries were duped and had to take the work off of their nonfiction shelves. He could have been put in jail. But you can still look up the cures in that book, and you could find copies of passages online, and it would seem to validate him. There's another one about bleaching. A bunch of people believes that you can cure autism with bleach because they believe autism is a microbial disease, not a neurological disorder. It's dangerous and an ongoing issue.

Right now, most people using the internet have some experience of life before the internet, or they're young enough that they're not basing major life decisions on what they learn on it. But in ten years, a large portion of the population is going to have grown up knowing only the internet as its only research tool. How are these folks going to be able to navigate just the amount of lies, propaganda, and bad advice that's out there? There's no way for them to understand how to go back and vet that information because they're going to have no experience of a world where it didn't exist.

Q: Before you transitioned into political consulting, you were an administrative librarian. How did those experiences as a public servant influence your future endeavors? What kind of guidance would you give to a young person considering a career in either library or political science?

A: I started as an elementary school librarian, which is hands down the best job in the entire world. That experience as an elementary school librarian is what guided my work in Sunnyvale, and Atherton, East Palo Alto, and elsewhere. Because I had that direct connection with those students, I saw the impact of reading on their lives from day-to-day. I saw them interact with books that were challenging and far beyond their reading level.

I had second and third graders reading the Harry Potter books, which is just amazing. If a second grader can get through the first book of Harry Potter, they're just going to read everything after that. It gave you confidence as a reader. Harry Potter was such a phenomenon that everybody was reading it, and you were only cool if you were reading it. It became this weird thing where it was uncool only to have watched the movies. You had to have read the books if you wanted to say you were a Harry Potter fan. So, kids were engaged in reading. Watching that transformation is what has guided me. My goal is to provide access to skills that can drastically improve the quality of these children's lives as they get older.

We just did a big research paper on crime statistics and library funding. Communities that spend more on library funding, literacy, and education have a lower crime rate and a much higher economic success rate. Those are economically viable communities. Some reports have come out that show libraries are one of the public expenditures that lead to a better quality of life and a happier life in those communities. Just enjoying seeing that happen firsthand is absolutely why a career in the library science field might be rewarding for you.

Q: And what about the political side of that equation?

A: One of the things that we had at one of my libraries in East Palo Alto was an after-school program called Quest that kids struggling with literacy could enroll in. If you know the background behind East Palo Alto, it was a tough neighborhood. It's the city that "Dangerous Minds" is about.

Well, when I first took my job there, they were putting window tinting on my office window, and I asked them why. Does the sun come up over there or something? They said no, it's bulletproof. That's the environment that I walked into. But at this school, at the Quest program, this second grader came in. He was refusing to read. He didn't have a male role model at home. His mother worked two jobs. His father was incarcerated. His brother had been killed by gang violence. He was failing out of second grade.

So, he got enrolled in Quest. We taught him the sight words is, and, or, the, that. Once he picked those up, he became a very confident reader. It's a magical shortcut to reading for a lot of these kids. Once they've identified these words, reading becomes more manageable, and the challenging words feel less demanding.

He wound up reading through all of our historical fiction books, through second, third, fourth grade. Then he got into our historical nonfiction books and read through all those. He came back as a tutor in high school, wound up getting a scholarship, and a history degree at Stanford. Witnessing that kind of impact on his life is what drove me to political science and action. Also, during the recession, when I had to lay off half my staff and cut our library hours, I learned that library funding is entirely political. Ninety-eight percent of library funding across the country is political. Only two percent are philanthropic grants and small donations.

So that's what led to me becoming involved in politics. And I would say don't do it unless you're utterly passionate about it. This is work that will burn you out fast unless you care, and you're in it for the long term.

Chapter 17

Strengthening Protection and Embracing Connections

Douglas C. Williams, CEO, Williams Data
Topics: Business Continuity, Civic Responsibility

"The future belongs to the fleet of foot. So, guess what, those with a fixed mindset will be passed over by those with a growth mindset."
Doug Williams

Douglas C. Williams is CEO of Williams Data Management and Chairman of the Board for the Vernon Chamber of Commerce. He has over 30 years of experience helping Fortune 500 clients with their document storage, destruction, and data security needs. He earned his bachelor's in broadcast communications from San Francisco State University.

Q: Doug, your family has been involved in the data management business for the better part of a century, and you've seen a lot of players come and go. How do small businesses like Williams remain resilient in the disruptive world of digital transformation, and what should executives be thinking about in terms of their long-term information management strategies?

A: Commercial records management, the holistic approach at 30,000 feet includes the digital component, as well as the legacy hard copy component. Our transition in the early 1980s into the commercial records center business from industrial freight warehousing and distribution witnessed similar disruptions. Those disruptions had mostly to do with the shift to the service economy from the industrial and manufacturing economies. Our client base includes enterprise size businesses as well as small and medium-sized businesses.

Executives in charge of information assets need to recognize the holistic scope of those information assets, whether they are structured or unstructured, and apply the information governance and regulatory guidelines to each equally. Knowing that digital technologies will change at light-speed, CEOs and their executive teams need to be knowledgeable and ready for changes in forensic discovery and see the impact of retention milestones for each type of information asset. We all know that text messages, email, and all social media posts have a permanent residency somewhere. Every business, large or small, has to accept a contingent liability regarding them. They need to recognize the action of maintaining a strict policy regarding their information management policies, irrespective of the resident media.

Q: You were interviewed by Adam Burroughs of Smart Business Los Angeles and highlighted a growing alarm over data breaches. Here we are just a few years later, and data protection is a daily news flash. Do you still feel the majority of organizations are taking security and privacy for granted, or are you now starting to see a trend toward proactive management of data?

A: I do. They are taking for granted, it won't happen to them, and if it does, they are insured. But guess what, that is delusional. Again, a proactive plan requires a holistic approach to information management. The IT department knows how to protect the data, but typically do not know the why, like what are the governing rules for each type of data. That is the province of the CIO or the Director of Information Governance, or the General Counsel if an enterprise-size firm.

The breaches in the headlines are preventable; however, because of human errors in social media, emails, texts, data sharing, lack of encryption, and the like, entryways into personal information data sets are vulnerable. In our case at

Williams Data Management, because we are social media users, we installed front end data intrusion software, pioneered and patented by Oasis Technologies, known as TITAN, which blocks over half-a-million intrusions attempts per week from getting into our networks.

Firewalls help, but TITAN's magic has been 'swatting away' the attempts for over 30 years. Proactive, yes. Ongoing, yes. The recognition by executives that they hold personally identifiable information (PII) is step one in creating an IG plan to protect an organization from data breaches. Then the next step is to assess the business vulnerabilities and create a system that enables a security culture. Our firm has partnered with CSR Professional Services, Inc., which provides our clients with a suite of data breach tools enabling business continuity readiness and breach notification services in all 50 states, and in the EU as well.

Q: You embarked on some big community and public service projects by taking the helm at the Vernon Chamber of Commerce. How has your experience in the private sector prepared you for developing and influencing public-private partnerships, and what do you see as the most defining aspect of those types of engagements?

A: Yes, it is my personal goal at Vernon Chamber of Commerce to enable business and government, working together, to create growth mindsets. The future belongs to the fleet of foot. So, guess what, those with a fixed mindset will be passed over by those with a growth mindset. For example, the 21st century, now nearly 20 percent over, is for the information economy. It's for using data, software, and robotics for manufacturing and distribution. It is no longer a labor vs. capital economy. It is a labor vs. technology economy.

In my opinion, and it is happening now, government entities using taxpayer dollars should either fund economically feasible growth mindset manufacturing projects in California or lower the taxes of growth mindset businesses, so they have the funds to do these projects themselves. Either way, the beneficiary population will win. Private sector leaders know projects must be profitable. Elected leaders must recognize the same thing. A public-private project must be profitable and self-sustaining, to enable the public to trust they'll earn a return on the capital spend. The era of never-ending funding of boondoggle "bridge to nowhere" projects is over. The Vernon Chamber of Commerce has embraced a growth mindset, and that is why I decided to lead it.

Q: For years, you've chaired an annual breakfast to support goodwill efforts in Israel and across the Middle East. You started this as a small gathering, and it has grown into one of the Jewish National Fund's biggest events. Why is corporate social responsibility so cardinal to you, and how has that awareness changed the way you approach running your business?

A: Corporate responsibility starts with the people who own it. In the case of the Jewish National Fund, which has existed since 1903, the task of communicating its mission to Los Angeles was easy. And year after year for 12 years, we at JNF-Los Angeles provided an annual educational program. I called it the Annual Executive Briefing to bring in Israeli leaders to speak about current events, policy plans, and the like, in a breakfast gathering. The format was very successful in Los Angeles, and that format was scaled nationally. JNF has scores of cities with annual breakfast events now. As it grew in Los Angeles, we asked for corporate sponsorships to underwrite the cost of the event enabling every attendee a free ticket to attend. I felt it was vitally important not to charge attendees for breakfast. I still feel that way. If an attendee wants to make a gift, that is welcome, but we at JNF wanted to grow the knowledge of the importance of Israel within the Los Angeles community, free of charge.

Our speakers over the years have included Ambassadors, elected officials, authors, political commentators, and members of the Israel Knesset. In the dozen-plus years, the event has been going in Los Angeles, attendance has totaled well over a thousand people per year, and it raises almost a million annually.

Q: You graduated with a Broadcast Journalism degree but ended up running a successful data management company! If you could go back in time and change your focus to a different major, do you think it would still lead you to your ultimate destination? What kind of advice might you give somebody at a similar fork in the road?

A: Well, that's a LOL! Personal evolution is all about a growth mindset. In the 1970s, I was not thinking about records and information management. The Broadcast Journalism direction was, I recall, a result of my taste for policy, economics, and communications. I thought I could be the next Dan Rather or Roger Mudd. If those names resonate, you are my age. Journalism was news writing with a focus on facts and consequences. Nowadays, not as much. My advice is the same as Yogi Berra's, who said, 'When you get to the fork in the road, take it!" By that, I think he meant to do what your passion and intelligence say to you is correct. Fuel your passion and do it to the best of your ability, whatever it is. Be happy and content with your lot. It is not greener on the other side; it is just on the other side.

Chapter 18

The Future of Compliance

Miguel Mairlot, Partner, Ethikos Lawyers
Topics: Compliance, Data Protection

"To build a strong compliance program, it is of utmost importance to work towards good communication with regulators."
Miguel Mairlot

Miguel Mairlot is an attorney and Data Protection Officer (DPO) with a breadth of compliance experience advising wealth management and insurance businesses. He has written and spoken extensively about compliance topics and teaches financial law in Brussels, Belgium. Miguel completed his undergraduate work at Université Catholique de Louvain and received his advanced master's in business law from Ghent University.

Q: Miguel, how did you find yourself gravitating towards the universe of finance and compliance?

A: Finance has always fascinated me because it is so dependent on the idea, the value of trust. Without investor confidence and trust in financial institutions, there is no room for innovation and growth. It is the trust we afford each other that allows our businesses to grow and our economies to flourish. One of the objectives of compliance is to maintain public confidence in the financial system. The compliance mechanism requires financial institutions to put in place, under penalty of sanctions, a whole series of preventive mechanisms that contribute to the achievement of this crucial objective. Rather than focusing on quick wins, compliance favors a long-term vision that focuses on sustaining our economies.

I spent the first ten years of my career working in litigation, specializing in banking and finance laws. My expertise and knowledge of the Markets in Financial Instruments Directive (MiFID) led me to work on its implementation for various financial institutions. At that time, legal and compliance tasks were usually performed by the same department. Although I'm still interested and continue working on several aspects of that regulation, I devote most of my time on issues related to money laundering and the detection of serious tax fraud in the event of repatriation of assets.

Q: How do you think companies should approach the challenges of implementing the European Union's General Data Protection Requirement?

A: Any company subject to GDPR should take care when implementing the requirements set out by this new regulation. Before its entry into force, data protection was not a top priority for European companies. Now the paradigm is about to change, due mainly to the hefty fines which can be imposed and the potential reputation damages which may result from a violation of the provisions. Among all these tasks, raising awareness among employees about the risks related to the infringement of the rules set out by GDPR might constitute the biggest challenge since this new piece of legislation is also considered a cultural change in Europe. The implementation of GDPR will require the revision of internal procedures, the appointment of a Data Protection Officer in some cases, and a mapping and assessment of all the data processes, as well as contractual changes.

Q: New York State introduced the Stop Hacks and Improve Data Electronic Security Act (SHIELD) bill, which among other things, updates breach notification requirements. There have also been global and stateside efforts to pass bills similar to the EU's "Right to be Forgotten" requirements. Given some of the geopolitical shifts around the world, do you see support for these regulations increasing or waning?

A: The expansion of the legislative rules which took place in Europe since the last financial crisis has no precedent. Complying with all the national and European laws and regulations has become increasingly complex and costly for companies. Data protection does not necessarily constitute an exception to those rules. GDPR provisions were heatedly debated before the European Commission during the drafting process, and this text constitutes the last bastion that protects European data users against their potential abusers.

The court decisions made during the last few years by the European Court of Justice, namely Maximillian Schrems v Data Protection Commissioner; and Google v Spain seem to be in line with this trend. For these reasons, I believe that any change in the data protection regulations that dramatically reduces the rights of the data users would call into question the democratic legitimacy of some of our institutions.

Q: The Financial Services and Markets Authority (FSMA) is one of the two authorities, along with the National Bank of Belgium (NBB), entrusted with the supervision of the Belgian financial sector. In the United States, it is FINRA, the Financial Industry Regulatory Authority, and the Securities Exchange Commission, or SEC, that is responsible for ensuring compliance in our financial institutions and markets. What do you see as the challenges in working with these groups?

A: To build a strong compliance program, it is of utmost importance to work towards good communication with regulators. Since last year, any individual employed in the financial sector who observes an infringement against the financial legislation rules which the FSMA is responsible for enforcing can report it directly to the FSMA. The whistleblower's identity is kept secret, and the law protects any individual who, in good faith, reported the infringement.

Even if we can be pleased about this recent development, regulators should also have sufficient staff to perform, on a risk-basis, on-site controls. Even while encouraging cooperation, they need to exercise their ability to impose sanctions in the event of non-compliance. Otherwise, it becomes difficult to convince any employee or management team about the importance of complying with applicable rules and regulations if the regulators never impose a noticeable sanction.

Q: How should financial institutions approach introducing AI and robots into their environments, and will it have a positive impact on compliance in the long term?

A: Financial institutions have been leveraging those kinds of tools to detect suspicious transactions related to money laundering and identifying counterparties subject to sanctions for a while. Some of them already make use of predictive models. The use of AI or robotics may present opportunities for financial institutions if certain tasks or low-risk decisions can be automated using these new technologies. In addition to being cost-effective, these solutions could improve the efficiency of a compliance monitoring program and help mitigate risks. However, I seriously doubt that, at least for now, regulators would agree that the most material compliance tasks should be entrusted to an AI tool or any form of robotics, mainly for liability purposes. To my knowledge, no robot has been held responsible yet by a regulator or a court for a violation of a legal provision.

Q: What is your advice for young professionals, millennials, entering, and trying to succeed in the fields of privacy, risk, and compliance?

A: I would advise them first to question their ethics. What is your take on issues like money laundering, sanctions, the fight against terrorism, or data protection, for instance? Compliance offers the opportunity to perform a job in a more preventive and efficient way than ever before. Within an organization, your decisions will often be challenged by the sales or product department, which does not always understand the underlying issues that can be raised by certain unethical or illegal behaviors. For these reasons, it is healthy to keep a long-term vision to achieve sustainability while ensuring business growth. If you have and believe in that vision, embrace the challenges and opportunities that come.

Chapter 19

Turning Collective Wisdom into Strength

Andrea Kalas, VP of Archives, Paramount Pictures
Topics: Digital Archives, Library Science

"If there's one thing I admire the most among the younger members of our field, it is their dedication to recognizing the path that is the worthiest... to their colleagues, to the collections, to the world they work and live in."
Andrea Kalas

Andrea Kalas is a former President of the Association of Moving Image Archivists (AMIA) and a member of the Academy of Motion Picture Arts and Sciences (AMPAS). Before her current role as SVP of Archives at Paramount Pictures, she led the preservation program at the British Film Institute. She received her bachelor's in film from Temple University and finished her master's in film at the University of California at Los Angeles.

Q: Andrea, we now exist in a world of accessible digital archives, but this new paradigm has ushered in an entirely new set of preservation challenges. You've spoken and taught at length about one of them, bit loss, and how it affects the race to preserve not just America's rich film history, but the cinematic treasures around the world. How does a global team like yours prioritize its goals as it races against the clock?

A: Digital preservation has the basic goal of avoiding bit loss, technically. However, the work that requires technologists and archivists to collaborate effectively involves the treatment of files as valuable records, art, or artifacts. This goes against so much of how basic information technology systems work. For example, the word "archive" has been used as a term to mean data written off-line and put on removable media on a shelf, never to be touched again. This is a sure path to bit loss. For an archivist, this definition is counterproductive. It as much about communication and clear technical requirements from archivists as it is building technical solutions.

What we've developed is an infrastructure that makes sure there are multiple copies of our feature films, and that each file that makes up that film is checked annually. We've also worked hard at making sure that we've architected things so that as hardware and software change, which they inevitably do, the files and metadata that make up that film can survive. This keeps us on track with what we have to preserve. That and the incredibly brilliant archivists who work with me and bring innovation to the process as it evolves.

Q: Beyond the importance of posterity in the arts, what are the benefits of preservation for large intellectual property firms like those in the entertainment business?

A: Entertainment companies base their business plans on the ability to distribute films and television programs over the long-term and benefit from the preservation of their intellectual property both financially and culturally. The cultural aspect is often called in business terms, "branding," or the public recognition of the value of that company. A film studio that demonstrates it cares as much about a film that has excellent public and cultural appreciation as it has financial benefit enhances its brand. These two reasons are why those who own intellectual property have a duty of care. We have some titles we distribute for a short period and others for which we have long-term rights. It is the latter we preserve.

Q: Much of the credit for modern advances in artificial intelligence goes to academics like Fei-Fei Li at Stanford, who built large image data sets. Now we're seeing software vendors developing tools for visual asset management that integrate machine learning to auto-classify large volumes of assets. Are solutions like this on the horizon for organizations like yours?

A: I'm excited about the tools that are available to archivists based on the incredible advances in this field. One of the quotes I use from Fei Li is "human values define machine values." To me that not only reminds me of her guidance on how to include all types of humans in interpretation, it also points to the phenomenal work of so many in the field of library science who have spent over a century on concepts like classification and subject headings which address the same challenge: how to bring structure to a collection of knowledge.

Perhaps it is happening somewhere, but I have yet to see an AI demonstration from the companies who are selling this service say, "and we've incorporated the Library of Congress standards on motion picture genres." We can and should continue to argue about the way a definition is assigned to any one object, but why haven't the machines learned from the humans who have already done a lot of research around these kinds of definitions? I'd love to see that.

Q: As we welcome a new generation of librarians, archivists, and data professionals, what are you observing in terms of their attitudes towards these roles given their upbringing in a wholly digital world? What positive qualities are we seeing in these individuals that separate them from the pack?

A: Maybe the cliché millennial is not attracted to archiving, but those who I have worked with in that age group have only taught me how to be open to new ideas; how to collaborate; how to use algorithms to solve mundane problems so we can all concentrate on the more significant issues. I feel lucky to be challenged by intelligent people, no matter their age or demographic designation. If there's one thing I admire the most among the younger members of our field, it is their dedication to recognizing the path that is the worthiest, to their colleagues, to the collections, to the world they work and live in.

Q: One of our goals here is to identify common themes that run across all cultures and shared disciplines. Is there one concept or rule you feel is ubiquitous across the records, data, and archives landscape?

A: I think for the past 25 years, or so our heads have been down as we've been trying to bridge an analog-to-digital transition. That's given us an incredible perspective on legacy approaches, legacy systems, and legacy decisions against how new technologies and techniques can completely change our work. It's time to lift our heads and look around and talk to each other. I'm so glad you are doing this through this series of interviews. Although we need to be experts in our corner of the field – legal, entertainment, historical records, corporate governance, we need each other now more than ever to discover where our collective wisdom can turn into a strength.

Q: What guidance would you give a person just beginning their career in library science, archiving, and data governance or thinking about a career transition?

A: I have a very tired joke about what it takes to work in the Paramount Archives. Study *Sunset Boulevard* as hard as you study Unix. The point is to start with the collection and the work you have in front of you. Find what it is about it that is fascinating. Is it silent films from India? Is it how systems can work together better because you see connections others don't? My too-often repeated piece of advice is to make sure this is the field you want to work in because of the people working in it. I've been able to meet some fair-minded, innovative people who think a little like me. Many are long-time friends. I'm grateful for that.

Chapter 20

Finding Genuine Talent in an Artificial World

Erick Swain, Practice Director, Personify Executive Search

Topics: Recruitment, Human Resources, Professional Development

"Employers need to be able to ask specific questions, drill-down, and recover the root causes of problems and fill those gaps. We do not minimize skill sets by any stretch, but we have also learned that the 'intangible' side of the equation gives both sides a better shot at a long-term fit."

Erick Swain

Erick Swaine is a practice director for Mackenzie Ryan, a global talent recruiting firm and specializes in information governance, AI, and analytics. He has placed thousands of job candidates across a broad spectrum of industries into mid-level to executive leadership positions and frequently speaks on their journeys and the mechanics of professional development. He earned his bachelor's in marketing from the University of North Carolina at Chapel Hill.

Q: Erick, you were an early pioneer in helping employers understand the value and talent that information governance, AI, and analytics professionals offered when these disciplines were in their infancy. How has the demand for these emerging fields transformed recruiting in the job market?

A: There's a lot to unpack there as it relates to tech itself, the demand for these emerging fields, and how that has transformed over the years. I come from the industry myself. Prior to my current role, I sold analytics software with built-in compliance and document management capabilities. Our firm recognized value in analytics and was looking to build a technology practice. Mackenzie Ryan, which split off from Personify last year (both held under Mackenzie Ryan Holdings), didn't have it when I came abroad, so they went to their private equity VC partners and asked them, "Where are you investing as it relates to technology?" There was a resounding theme around electronically stored information. This was about a dozen years ago.

At that point, not everyone had a content management system. The players were SharePoint, OpenText, and OnBase and companies like Stellent, which was later picked up by Oracle, and FileNet, which was picked up by IBM. But they hadn't penetrated all the markets. Early on, the investment was in Content Management and overall repositories. It was soup-to-nuts storage of data, you know, manipulating workflows for all components of information management.

Overall, human capital demand is there because of the efficiency that you can create by understanding your data. The newfound efficiency is driving advanced analytics and AI over the last five to six years, with massive amounts of investments around how we make decisions around these resources. This strategy requires the right talent.

As companies started to evolve, and you had social media come into play, around the same time, there were massive amounts of electronically stored data being created. Although storage kept getting cheaper and cheaper, there was a lot of regulation coming out requiring governance of data. They looked at the discipline of information governance as a cost only and then hopped over into advanced analytics. Over the last three or four years, they have moved into artificial intelligence.

Yet, it's all about making sense of the data that we're already storing, and probably not defensibly disposing of. What the new technology has done for both large and small employers is to allow these companies to make data-driven decisions, and they drive those decisions based on a lot of historical legacy data. We noticed there are several companies that either used advanced analytics platforms or AI for internal knowledge management (to enhance institutional knowledge and train their people better), or they began aggregating and analyzing the data to develop additional revenue streams externally.

Q: Do we have enough of the right types of candidates? For example, insurance companies can't seem to find enough people who understand telematics because the technology is so new in and of itself.

A: That's certainly the case in some respects. You take machine learning, deep learning, or natural language processing. There's certainly a limited talent pool there. AI is a field that's just a few years old, and so to go in and ask someone for three to five years' experience is very tough. As a result, organizations have grown these capabilities internally and certified their own people around those programs. Yet, there remains an absolute shortage in many different related areas.

Good data scientists, for example, can be hard to find. Certain developers are moving away from traditional skillsets, and into the open-source world, so we see a shortage of talent there. Employers need to be able to ask specific questions, drill-down, and recover the root causes of problems and fill those gaps. We do not minimize skill sets by any stretch, but we have also learned that the 'intangible' side of the equation (i.e., personality, culture, management style, etc.) gives both sides a better shot at a long-term fit.

Q: Due to the speed of technology, how are HR departments dealing with succession planning in their IT groups now that it's the case that what's needed in a successor is not simply soft skills and pedigrees,

*but working knowledge of systems and programming languages that
are still burgeoning?*

A: We are seeing the focus is on employee engagement and
employee retention. There are a lot of strategies being built
around this capability. For example, a lot of the data we look at,
especially with the sub-four percent or so employment rate, is
evidence that it's tough now in this climate to find exceptional
talent. What it comes down to is succession plans have to be built
through an understanding of your organization by engaging
your employees, and through that engagement process,
companies learn the motivations of their staff, understand when
big events happen, and how it affects certain departments. By
understanding and gleaning information around that, they're
able to get in front of situations that may cause challenges to a
succession plan.

You'll also hear quite a bit about employee analytics, and these
systems are helping management understand trends and predict
problems that may be prevented earlier. We use them ourselves,
and also provide them to our clients. We believe, again, that it's
not only just about attracting talent. It's often more critical these
days to think about the employees that are already in the seat,
and how you will retain them. That's what we see as the decisive
factor to a lot of employers. That factor is especially true in the
tech world because there's not just a battle for talent; there's a
war.

The war is not only on understanding bigger, faster, stronger
systems but also on culture. If you could understand that, it's
kind of like the old metaphor of bottling up lightening. If you
could bottle that up and understand it, and then put the systems
into place to watch the outliers, then you're able to predict
succession plans better. This strategy helps you predict when
and where you may need help because you're watching the data
insights behind employee engagement.

Q: What about the fact that some folks don't expect to work at a place for 20 or 30 years anymore? What are the drivers that keep people around nowadays besides compensation?

A: Drivers can be a multitude of things. However, it comes down to timing. So, what we are looking at is where these individuals are in the trajectory of their careers. Are they just starting out, or are they five years in looking for promotion to climb the ladder? Are they ten years in, have kids? Knowing where they give you a better understanding of what their motivations are. When you know what their motivations are, it helps you with your planning and satisfying those needs. You must make sure to drive your decisions by understanding why that individual is motivated, and the way that they're motivated, at that given time. A lot of companies are building structures around that idea, from wellness programs to empowering committee structures, to doing charity work.

Q: There's also a lot of talk about burnout. What do you think are the drivers for that?

A: There's a couple of pieces around burnout. The ones that we see a lot of the time is when companies have less of an idea around their vision. They change direction a lot. We've noticed it when there is no management to help communicate and assist with the change. That creates this kind of 8000 RPM running mode of all employees. It's hamster-wheel running. It's not running in a systematically scalable direction. More bureaucracy, red tape, not being able to get things done creates burnout as well.

Q: Are you talking about a change in business strategy like a company redirecting its revenue stream or introducing a new business model?

A: Yes, like a company going from on-prem to Cloud, that type of transformation. Or transforming a services company into a software company. Institutional transformation with a lack of planning, execution, and communication around the change is where we see a lot of burnout happen.

Q: *How has recruitment process outsourcing or RPO influenced the candidate selection process, and does it result in employees staying longer in a chosen position?*

A: I'm on the executive search side, but I know a lot about the recruitment process outsourcing side as well. The way that it influences the candidate selection process depends on how in-depth their RPO is. If they're handling everything A to Z, RPO is beneficial from branding the website, running the back end, posting all the positions, and managing all the incoming candidates. It helps, but it comes down to making sure candidates have a good experience. That's what we've noticed over time. It's what the recruiting industry has unfortunately fallen short of at times. For example, have you ever had a recruiter call you and then not called you back after they said they would? That type of experience has an impact on an organization.

To counter that, we run all the efficiencies so that every touchpoint is covered. So, our influence is mainly on experience. That's what an RPO does. It's about the authentic candidate experience. In our RPO clients, everyone gets a callback. The first candidate and second candidates are surveyed, along with the candidate that got the job and the manager. This strategy allows us to have continual process improvement.

Does it result in an employee staying longer? When we use the engagement factor we talked about, it certainly does. When we have the recruitment process outsourcing, put into play, and then on top of that, we have engagement software that delights the employee. We're able to have a seamless integration starting at onboarding. Also, as they are three months in, six months in, whatever cadence, you set up a regular check-in with that employee. When that happens, we've seen data to support the fact that placements are staying longer in a chosen position and seem happier.

Q: We often overuse the maxim, "Do what you love," which is easier said than done. Is there any career advice you'd have for a new college graduate, or a person between jobs, trying to find the right spot? For example, how long do you wait for the right gig?

A: I work with SKEMA, S-K-E-M-A, which is an international business school at NC State. I go there through a couple of our programs that we run at the firm and speak to grad students. My advice to them is about understanding yourself first. If you can know your why, if you can understand why you do the things that you do, you're moving in the right direction. Like the organizational consultant Simon Sinek says, people don't buy what you do. They buy why you do it.

I genuinely know I can affect change in someone's career, and I take it very seriously. If they allow me to sit down and get to know them, not from just the skill set perspective, but truly an intangible aspect. What are their drivers? Is it a challenge? Is it money? Is it advancement? What are the things that drive them, given where they are in their current circumstances? If I can understand that, and if these individuals coming out of college can understand what's important to them right now, then they're better equipped to put themselves in the position to seize the right opportunity.

Q: You've coached softball for Special Olympics now for a couple of decades. What has that organization and its athletes taught you about teamwork and success in general, that you might convey to somebody building their resume or their career?

A: I've coached Special Olympics softball for 16 years, and I probably get way more out of it than they do. In essence, it's teamwork. I have had to reteach my team, certain members of the team, certain skills every year. It teaches patience. We all learn comradery and love for one another. It's not what it's about whatsoever, but we got walloped all the time. I mean, we went seven years straight without winning a game, okay?

Finally, one year we started winning and got into the last tournament game, so we were going for the gold. Long story short, we lost, and much of the team doesn't know if we win or lose. So, they came up to me and said, "Coach, coach, hey, did we win? Did we win?" And I turned around to them, and I was like, "You know we're all winners, we're going home with some hardware, we got second place." A few minutes later, I was talking to one of the coaches, and I hear right behind me, suddenly, this chant, "We're number two! We're number two!" They're all celebrating. And I just lost it. I mean, that is to me what it's all about. I was like, these athletes are so genuine, and this is as good as it gets.

We ended up winning in the 50th anniversary last year, after all those kinds of tough years, so it was cool to see our athletes, some of whom I've had the whole time, mark that accomplishment. You know, it's all the little things. It's a theme in what we're talking about today. If we learn people, that's where you get to listen and actively listen. In all walks, right? When I'm listening to a candidate, when I'm listening to a client, when a new grad student is listening to a professor, or listening to someone, they're interviewing with, when we're listening to our children, when we're listening to our parents, that's when the meaningful stuff happens.

It comes down to the intangibles I've noticed in this people business. When you understand someone at that level and understand what their motivation and their drivers are, you can truly build a team, and a very successful team, especially when you have a high-care quotient around it as well.

Epilogue

As we bravely march through the upheaval of the Information Age, our hopes for the workforce outnumber our worries and concerns.

This optimism is deeply seeded in a repeated meditation that the will of the achiever knows no obstacle it cannot face and eventually overcome. These original interviews document professional challenges, but they are also evidence of real success. Success through discipline. Success through study. Success through valuing wisdom derived not merely from our education and experience but passed down to us from our respected peers. That's why we positively expect the leaders profiled in this book to emerge as defining voices in the future's global digital disruption, innovation, and governance discussions. We already know their goodwill has made a tangible difference in lives like ours and hope it will work in yours as well.

We can't know exactly what the jobs of the future will look like, but the chances are that both the technical and soft skills examined in this book will serve as a basis for their qualifications. Like the leaders profiled in these chapters, each of us has a valuable contribution to make to that future and each other. We are an intricate species whose faults are well documented, but whose many inspired gifts and evergreen qualities are yet to be tapped. Your next step is leveraging those gifts when the opportunity arises, doing so strategically, and with the aid of the friends, family, and colleagues that make life worth living.

About the Authors

Rafael Moscatel is an award-winning Information Governance Professional (IGP), Certified Records Manager (CRM) and *Certified Information Privacy Manager* (CIPM). He has decades of experience developing large-scale information management and digital transformation programs for Fortune 500 companies, including Paramount Pictures and Farmers Insurance. In 2015, he partnered with Stanford University and produced The Little Girl with the Big Voice, an acclaimed documentary based on historical archives and the Doctrine of Fair Use. He was honored with the Excellence for an Organization Award by ARMA International and regularly speaks at industry conferences about the evolving discipline of IG, including the AIIM Conference, BoxWorks, the International Legal Technology Association, the MER Conference, and the Document Strategy Forum. He is available for speaking engagements, consulting opportunities, and interviews.

Abby Moscatel is a California trial attorney for State Farm Mutual Automobile Insurance Company. She combines her love for the law and passion for emerging technology by writing and presenting on ethics and admissibility of evidence related to IoT and social media. She obtained her JD from Southwestern Law School's accelerated SCALE program and her BS in Legal Communication from Ohio University. Before law school, Abby was based in Washington, D.C., where she helped pioneer the use of the internet to mobilize students nationwide to lobby for increased access to federal financial aid. She also previously handled media relations for the Ohio Senate Democratic Caucus through the Ohio Legislative Service Commission's fellowship program. Abby was the executive producer on Rafael's *The Little Girl with the Big Voice*, assisting with the story editing, copyright licensing, and crowd-funding necessary to produce and distribute the film.

Rafael and Abby's first careers will always be Mom and Dad. They live in Los Angeles with their beloved children and dog named Pikachu Elsa.

From the Authors

Thank you for purchasing *Tomorrow's Jobs Today: Wisdom and Career Advice from Thought Leaders in AI, Big Data, Blockchain, the Internet of Things, Privacy, and More.* Our sincere hope is that you derived as much from reading this book as we have in creating it. If you have a few moments, please feel free to add your review of the book to your favorite online site for feedback. Please visit our website for news on upcoming works, recent blog posts, and to sign up for our newsletter: www.tomorrowsjobstoday.com.

Business Books

Business Books publishes practical guides
and insightful non-fiction for beginners and professionals.
Covering aspects from management skills, leadership and
organizational change to positive work environments, career
coaching and self-care for managers, our books are a valuable
addition to those working in the world of business.

15 Ways to Own Your Future
Take Control of Your Destiny in Business and in Life
Michael Khouri
A 15-point blueprint for creating better collaboration, enjoyment,
and success in business and in life.
Paperback: 978-1-78535-300-0 ebook: 978-1-78535-301-7

The Common Excuses of the Comfortable Compromiser
Understanding Why People Oppose Your Great Idea
Matt Crossman
Comfortable compromisers block the way of anyone trying to
change anything. This is your guide to their common excuses.
Paperback: 978-1-78099-595-3 ebook: 978-1-78099-596-0

The Failing Logic of Money
Duane Mullin
Money is wasteful and cruel, causes war, crime and dysfunctional
feudalism. Humankind needs happiness, peace and abundance. So
banish money and use technology and knowledge to rid the world
of war, crime and poverty.
Paperback: 978-1-84694-259-4 ebook: 978-1-84694-888-6

Mastering the Mommy Track
Juggling Career and Kids in Uncertain Times
Erin Flynn Jay
Mastering the Mommy Track tells the stories of everyday working
mothers, the challenges they have faced, and lessons learned.
Paperback: 978-1-78099-123-8 ebook: 978-1-78099-124-5

Modern Day Selling
Unlocking Your Hidden Potential
Brian Barfield
Learn how to reconnect sales associates with customers and unlock
hidden sales potential.
Paperback: 978-1-78099-457-4 ebook: 978-1-78099-458-1

The Most Creative, Escape the Ordinary, Excel at Public
Speaking Book Ever
All The Help You Will Ever Need in Giving a Speech
Philip Theibert
The 'everything you need to give an outstanding speech' book,
complete with original material written by a professional speech-
writer.
Paperback: 978-1-78099-672-1 ebook: 978-1-78099-673-8

Readers of ebooks can buy or view any of these bestsellers
by clicking on the live link in the title. Most titles are published
in paperback and as an ebook. Paperbacks are available in
traditional bookshops. Both print and ebook formats
are available online.
Find more titles and sign up to our readers' newsletter at
http://www.jhpbusiness-books.com/
Facebook: https://www.facebook.com/JHPNonFiction/
Twitter: @JHPNonFiction